W9-COU-500

Thinking
of
You

Weddings
FLORISTS' REVIEW

FREESIA • LILAC • LEPTOSPERMUM • VIBURNUM • ASTILBE • FREESIA • LILAC • LEPTOSPERMUM

VIBURNUM • ASTILBE • FREESIA • LILAC • LEPTOSPERMUM • VIBURNUM • ASTILBE • FREESIA

LILAC • LEPTOSPERMUM • VIBURNUM • FREESIA • LILAC • LEPTOSPERMUM

VIBURNUM • ASTILBE • FREESIA • VIBURNUM • ASTILBE • FREESIA

LILAC • LEPTOSPERMUM • LEPTOSPERMUM

VIBURNUM • ASTILBE • ASTILBE • FREESIA

LILAC • LEPTOSPE • LEPTOSPERMUM

VIBURNUM • A • ASTILBE • FREESIA

LILAC • LEPTOSPE • LEPTOSPERMUM

VIBURNUM • ASTILBE • ASTILBE • FREESIA

LILAC • LEPTOSPERMUM • LEPTOSPERMUM

VIBURNUM • ASTILBE • FRE • UM • ASTILBE • FREESIA

LILAC • LEPTOSPERMUM • VI • LILAC • LEPTOSPERMUM

VIBURNUM • ASTILBE • FREESIA • URNUM • ASTILBE • FREESIA

LILAC • LEPTOSPERMUM • VIB • REESIA • LILAC • LEPTOSPERMUM

VIBURNUM • ASTILBE • FREESIA • LILAC • SPERMUM • VIBURNUM • ASTILBE • FREESIA

LILAC • LEPTOSPERMUM • VIBURNUM • ASTILBE • FREESIA • LILAC • LEPTOSPERMUM

VIBURNUM • ASTILBE • FREESIA • LILAC • LEPTOSPERMUM • VIBURNUM • ASTILBE • FREESIA

Weddings

FLORISTS' REVIEW

Frances Dudley, AAF

Talmage McLaurin, AIFD

PUBLISHER

Frances Dudley

EXECUTIVE EDITOR

Talmage McLaurin, AIFD

ART DIRECTOR

Michael C. Snell

COPY EDITOR

Sally M. Snell

PROOFREADER

Shelley Urban

FLOWER PHOTOGRAPHY

Stephen Smith
Mark Robbins

FASHION PHOTOGRAPHY

Daniel Ray
Joe Comick
Lon Murdick
Heribert Brehm

FLORAL DESIGN

Talmage McLaurin, AIFD

CONTRIBUTING DESIGNERS

Carolyn Shepard, AIFD
Randy Baehre, AIFD
Kelly Marble, AIFD
Bill Harper, AIFD
David Porterfield, AIFD
Curtis Godwin, AIFD
Terry Lanker

Rights to the photographs appearing in this book were granted courtesy of Elegant Bride and Florists' Review magazines.

ISBN 0-9654149-4-9

©1998, Florists' Review Enterprises, Inc.

All rights reserved. No part of this publication may be reproduced without prior permission of the publisher.

Florists' Review Weddings was designed and produced by Florists' Review Enterprises, Inc.; 3641 SW Plass; Topeka, Kansas 66611-2588

Text excerpted from Florists' Review magazine, written by David Coake, Editor-in-Chief and Shelley Urban, Managing Editor.

Printed in the United States by The John Henry Company; Lansing, Michigan.

Separations and Postscript services by Capital Graphics, Inc.; Topeka, Kansas.

Design and Typesetting by Shade of the Cottonwood, L.L.C.; Topeka, Kansas.

FOREWORD

resh flowers are the bride's personal signature for her wedding day. By virtue of their fragility, flowers are at once elusive and romantic. Nature's special gift that can never be duplicated, they symbolize life and fertility while adding fragrance and freshness to carefully chosen dresses and handsome tuxedos. While the wedding gown can be stored away and worn again decades later by a nostalgic daughter or granddaughter, the flowers are the enhancement for this day alone–captured only in fading photographs and memories. They express the personality of the bride and the theme of the wedding like nothing else.

Whether the wedding is a grand event that calls for formal florals or an understated ceremony beneath an arbor of blooming branches, the flowers will highlight the appropriate mood. And while seasonality should play a role in the overall ambiance of the day, with today's advanced growing methods and transportation, almost any flower can be available year-round with proper notice.

At *Florists' Review* magazine, we have been guiding professionals through the art of floristry for over a century. And creating beautiful wedding flowers for hopeful brides has been an important part of florists' mission since the inception of the trade. This book, filled with photographs from the magazine's wedding issues, is meant to enhance the relationship between a florist and bride in creating her personal floral signature.

Glossaries

Fall
W E D D I N G S

Winter
W E D D I N G S

Weddings

THROUGHOUT HISTORY

c. 1920 A bride holds a bouquet of orchids, lily-of-the-valley, and
maidenhair fern. Small clusters of orange blossoms adorn her
headdress. **OPPOSITE:** c. 1905 Vows are exchanged under a floral
bell and garlanded arch.

History of the
American Wedding

Flowers and foliage have been used to visually emphasize the joy and romance of weddings in almost every culture on earth. The first bridal bouquets were made of aromatic herbs to ward off evil spirits. Medieval brides wore garlands of fresh blossoms in their hair, hoping to make their marriages as sweet as flowers, and brides in Tudor England would eat gilded marigolds dipped in fragrant rose water for their purported aphrodisiac effect. Flowers came to symbolize purity, prosperity, and fertility.

THE VICTORIAN ERA: 1837-1901

The marriage of Queen Victoria of England to Prince Albert has influenced the modern marital ceremony more than any other event in history. Victoria's wedding, though rich in ceremonial pomp, was a clear departure from earlier, more extravagant, royal unions. Her gown was designed with the understated elegance of "rich white satin trimmed with orange flower blossoms. On her

head, she wore a wreath of the same blossoms over which, but not so to conceal her face, a beautiful veil of Honiton lace was thrown." Though bridal gowns of various hues remained, the ideal of the white wedding was set firmly in place.

After the ceremony, American brides continued to wear their gowns to balls and used the veil as a shawl. For those lucky enough to travel to England and be presented to the Queen, the entire wedding outfit, including a white floral bouquet, was the appropriate attire.

The Victorian bridal bouquet was composed of carefully selected flowers and foliage to express the bride's sentiment and emotion. The flowers came to symbolize the day and were used throughout her life as "her flowers." A variety of flowers were used, but the bridal bouquet was almost always white and was tied with a pastel ribbon.

In the early years of the Victorian era, a small round posy of mixed flowers held in a tight circle or arranged in concentric rings was the traditional bouquet. At this

time, the posy, often referred to as a tussie-mussie, was so petite that the bride held it in one hand along with an elaborately embroidered lace handkerchief. Generally, a tussie-mussie included fragrant foliage in addition to flowers. The form of the finished bouquet was almost always rounded. The Victorian language of flowers was employed in selecting appropriate flowers to symbolize the bride's feelings for the groom. As the century progressed, the tussie-mussie remained a popular bouquet form, although the size increased.

Toward the end of the Victorian era, the bridal bouquet became more elaborate. By the late 1880s, the bouquets had become so large that brides often carried white prayer books at the ceremony, and left the bouquet to be held during receptions.

As the bridal bouquet evolved from posy to spray, the "shower bouquet" emerged. Knotting graduated lengths and loops of narrow ribbons with small flower buds and cascading them from the central flower arrangement created the "shower." Often the "shower" of flowers, foliage, and ribbon covered the front of the bride's gown and cascaded almost to her feet. These bouquets would often weigh as much as 10 to 15 pounds. Eucharis lilies, lilies-of-the valley, orange blossoms, gardenias, and stephanotises, tied with rich corded white ribbon in long bows, was a popular floral combination for shower bouquets.

c. 1928 A beautiful bride, flanked on either side by two romantic arrangements, carries a shower bouquet. **OPPOSITE:** c. 1900 The bride carries a posy with a cascade of ribbon. Bridesmaids hold walking staffs or wicker baskets.

Flowers weren't reserved strictly for use in the bridal bouquet. Often, brides would attach flowers, garlands, wreaths, and bouquets to their dresses. Brides and bridesmaids often wore dresses looped with bouquets of roses or adorned with orange blossoms and myrtle. Other bouquet styles included muffs, fans, and Bibles virtually covered with flowers.

After the ceremony, the bride would give each bridesmaid a flower from her bouquet. In some instances, the bridal bouquet was constructed as a composite design of small groups of flowers tied with ribbons. When the ribbon was untied, each bridesmaid received a small bouquet. The bridesmaid who found a small gold ring hidden in her bouquet would become the next bride.

Flowers for bridesmaids were arranged to match the bride's flowers or gown. Some bridesmaids carried flowers to honor the colors of the bridegroom's military regiment with insignia ribbons tied into the flowers. Other fashions included attaching bouquets to Louis XV-style walking sticks or carrying pale satin slippers filled with flowers and tied with long ribbons that matched the dresses.

American brides of the Victorian era often wore long veils of lace secured to their hair with coronets of orange blossoms–either real, waxed, or carved of ivory. Head wreaths were often made of ivy leaves and myrtle blossoms or white deutzia flowers; geranium leaves and white roses, pansies, and ivy; or azaleas and primroses for spring.

Gentleman's boutonnieres, or buttonhole bouquets as they were known in the 19th century, were made of gardenias, tea roses, camellias, carnations, lilies-of-the-valley, or tuberoses. Half-blown cabbage or garden roses, backed by maidenhair fern, coleus leaf, or begonia leaf, were also popular choices.

Ceremony decorations could create elaborate, opulent settings. Floral arches attached to the end of every pew were popular in late 19th century churches. Where arches were not employed, clusters of flowers and ribbon were attached to pews, or a hedge of flowers was placed on either side of the center aisle and garlands were wound around columns. Recommended decorations also included roses and ivy twined about the pillars; garlands of roses festooned from pillar to pillar; a huge cross of white blooms, flanked on either side by the Greek monogram in the same blooms, above the altar; pyramids of growing flowers standing in beds on either side of the altar; or lilies, palms, and arums with bright colored blossoms at the base of the altar. The altar, organ, and window sills were covered in mosses richly decorated with flowers.

Floral decorations for home weddings transformed parlors into chapels. Aisles were created with ribbons and bouquets. Garlands of flowers, greens, and ribbon would grace the staircase. Floral arrangements in the form of wedding bells, monograms, lovers' knots, yokes, and horseshoes were displayed in highly visible areas such as above fireplace mantels, in front of mirrors, or

in the archways of bay windows. Thick garlands of flowers and greenery were loosely draped in chandeliers. A fresh flower bell marked where the ceremony would take place, with ribbons, streamers, and garlands of flowers radiating out of it. The clapper might have been a dove with a sprig of orange blossoms in its beak.

Potted orange trees and exotic tropical plants were used at both church and home weddings to screen the large blocks of ice needed to cool guests at summertime ceremonies. Three-tier wedding cakes were considered the most elegant. These were usually decorated with white sugar icing and natural flowers. Wedding favors of small floral bouquets were often given to guests.

c. 1920 The bride carries a lovely shower bouquet while her attendants hold bouquets rich with rose blossoms. **OPPOSITE:** c. 1920 The bride and her bridesmaids carry abundant shower bouquets of sweet peas.

Brides of the American frontier endured crop failures, cricket infestations, and droughts, but rituals of marriage continued to play a central role in their lives. Weddings were occasionally performed in a church if a town had been established or in a friend's home or even outdoors along a dusty wagon trail. The bride wore her best dress. If she wore a veil, it would be a shawl that could keep her warm as the cold winter nights approached. If the season was right, she might carry a bouquet of simple wildflowers gathered from a nearby meadow. The reception was a community-wide event and was often followed by a square dance.

ART NOUVEAU: 1890s-1910
The Art Nouveau movement in America influenced wedding and bridal fashions by featuring a very naturalistic style of design. Ornamental characteristics included flower buds, vines and tendrils, and insect wings. Lines appeared delicate and sinuous or infused with a powerful rhythmic and whip-like force. From clothing to floral containers, these images abounded. Japanese-style garden settings became popular at wedding receptions, and bouquets generally took on a softer, more natural, appearance.

THE NEW CENTURY: 1900-1914
Life in America in the 1900s began to change in dramatic ways. The Wright brothers successfully flew an airplane, and Frank Lloyd Wright's "prairie style" houses, and the California bungalows of Bernard Maybeck

influenced home designs. Though the Arts and Crafts movement turned away from Victorian ornamentation, the Victorians still largely influenced bridal designs.

Shower-style bouquets consisting of gardenias, cattleyas, lilies-of-the-valley, and farleyense greenery continued to be popular. Other bouquet styles included prayer book markers, "armful" bouquets that cascaded down the left arm, and hat basket flowers.

WORLD WAR I: 1914-1918
The weddings of Woodrow Wilson's daughters in the White House brought a fresh appearance to wedding design. Designs for brides and bridesmaids included shower arm bouquets, staff baskets or bridal resting baskets, shepherd's crooks, *directoire* staff, and bridal shoulder baskets, as well as a renewed interest in colonial design.

ART DECO: 1920-1940
For American weddings, the Art Deco movement resulted in designs that featured the adaptation of simple, clean shapes that often appeared to have a "streamlined" look. Clean, more stylized geometric wedding bouquets and arrangements began to appear, especially when the style became more established in the 1930s and 1940s.

A period of prosperity followed World War I, and women had a new place of power and independence in American society. Coco Chanel and her distinctive tubular, easy-to-wear, knee-length tunic dresses and bobbed hair became popular, as well as her short wedding dress worn just below the knee with a court train. Gowns were white, and veils bridged the Victorian tradition with the modern wedding of the 1920s.

Shower bouquets remained popular, but the tussie-mussie, also known as the "colonial bouquet" found a renewed popularity. The colonial bouquet of the new century was composed of a smaller assortment of flowers in a looser, less formal arrangement than its predecessor.

Wedding accessories such as kneeling benches, wedding gates, aisle posts, and candelabra were popular. The 1920s have been dubbed "The Era of Aspiration," with economic confidence a defining

c. 1915 This bride wears a large fan-like corsage of roses and sprengeri, called a corsage bouquet, on the front of her fur-trimmed traveling suit. **OPPOSITE:** c. 1930 This elegant bridesmaid displays a cascading bouquet of gerbera and gladioli.

quality. Showing one's wealth was the natural act of demonstrating success. It was common for the social elite to spend vast amounts of money on the decorations for weddings and parties during this period.

THE DEPRESSION YEARS: 1929-1940

With the stock market collapse of 1929, the frivolity and economic boom of the 1920s came crashing down. Americans found solace from everyday hardships in the Hollywood-made opulence and fantasy at movie houses. Though many brides had to make due with the best dress they had, bridal fashion took its inspiration from the glamorous movie images featured on the silver screen.

Advances in florists' tools enabled bridal bouquets to take the form of cascades, crescents, wedding rings, and Grecian fans. The cascade took its modern form of a pointed oval or teardrop. Other popular styles were arm bouquets of callas, solid round bouquets with dropped satellite clusters, Easter lily arm bouquets with garlands, bridal purses with flowers, prayer books with clusters of flowers, and garland-style bouquets. Bouquets were backed with ribbon, lace, satin, paper doilies, and even feathers. Flowers on cuff bouquets were attached directly to plain cuff bands.

Florists developed new and creative ways to feature flowers for the bride and her party. The corsage bouquet, hat and arm basket bouquets, Hawaiian leis, and stuffed callas emerged as creativity soared. Muffs continued to be popular, although the muffs of the 1930s were lighter than their predecessors.

Ring bearers carried designs that featured a single calla with a circle of five roses at its base wrapped by a bow. The ring was placed over the calla's spadix, where it rested on a bed of cotton.

Topiary trees of solid round balls or conical shapes on poles were used in the 1930s. Garlands connected one topiary to another.

Home weddings became increasingly popular, but many couples in the 1930s were married in elaborate ceremonies that took place in fancy hotels. One such wedding in San Francisco was described like this:

"Gardenias, hundreds of them, were used in an elaborate decoration for a recent smart wedding at the St. Francis Hotel by Sheridan & Bell. Pyramidal trees were placed in the entrance. On these were attached gardenias to give the appearance of gardenia 'trees.' A fountain at the right side was outlined at the base with white stocks and in back of it was a hedge covered with gardenias.

Down the long ceremony room, a silver cloth led to the altar, which was also covered with a silver cloth. Directly in back was a high background of green foliage on which were draped conventionalized garlands in festoons. On each end of the altar was a tall silver candlestick and in the center was a silver, seven-branch candelabrum around the base of which were massed lilies-of-the-valley. Between the candlesticks were small trees made solid of lilies-of-the-valley in silver pots."

WORLD WAR II: 1939-1945

With the onset of World War II, the U.S. Government restricted the use of anything that was considered superficial or unessential. The bridal industry was not exempt from these restrictions. During this time, sentimental favorites came back into fashion. Brides began incorporating something blue into wedding bouquets, double wedding rings for the bride and groom came back, and carriages became popular additions to many weddings because of gasoline rationing.

During wartime, many brides had to forsake traditional weddings, as engagements often lasted only days or weeks. Many weddings involved the military, and brides were often married at the army camp. Borrowing white wedding gowns to wear during the ceremony was considered an acceptable, and even patriotic, option. Other brides found that there was no time to plan to wear anything except their best suits. As acknowledged

c. 1943 An elegant bride is
escorted down the aisle carrying
a crescent-like bouquet of
gardenias and stephanotises.
Her veil is embellished with the
same flowers. **OPPOSITE:** c. 1942
A couple marries at an army
base during a wartime furlough.

in a wartime column in Vogue, "Weddings nowadays hang not on the bride's whim but on the decision of the groom's commanding officer."

Furlough brides were women who married servicemen on leave from the war. These weddings represented a tremendous business throughout the war years, and florists were encouraged to cater to the bride who might have only a few weeks, days, or even hours to arrange her wedding.

"Reports from army camps indicate that servicemen are heartily in favor of 'pretty weddings and picture-book brides.' It is remembered that to the soldier or sailor, his bride represents just about everything in the world he is fighting for–all the beauty and the old traditions and the right to personal happiness as well as the promise of a home to which he can return in some future peacetime. Consequently, he, as well as the bride, deserves and appreciates the memory of a lovely wedding."

Dress code restricted military women, even at weddings: "WAACs in uniform may be attendants at a wedding but may neither carry nor wear flowers while in uniform. A WAAC bride may wear her uniform at her own wedding but in such a case is not allowed flowers. However, a WAAC who is to be a bride or an attendant may still wear the long dress of which she had always dreamed if she so desires and may, of course, have any flowers to go with it.

The WAVES are never allowed out of uniform, expect by special permission from their commanding officers, with an official okay from the bureau of personnel in Washington, D.C. This means that a member of the WAVES who wishes to be married in the traditional white dress may apply for this special permission, as at her own wedding is the only time she is ever granted the privilege of being out of uniform. While in uniform, a member of the WAVES is never permitted to wear flowers but, as a bride or a bridal attendant, she may carry flowers."

Small, stylized bouquets of red, white, and blue flowers were a patriotic choice for military weddings.

POSTWAR YEARS: 1946-1959

Fueled by a post-war economic high and confidence in the future, Americans returned to traditional ideas of love and marriage. The figure of the woman was romanticized and elevated to couture height by designers such as Christian Dior.

Dior's "new look" was a modern reinterpretation of 19th-century style, and brides readily adapted it to wedding fashion. From dainty baskets of daisies to regal fans clustered with orchids, the wedding flower fashion forecast promised an exciting selection of designs.

Wedding bouquets tended to be more angular and geometric with the addition of strings of pearls, glittered netting, bells of stiffened lace, chenille hearts, and fabric and maline leaves. Asymmetrical, cascade, and round bouquets were all present, but the most popular style tended to be the crescent, as it adapted well to the numerous embellishments available.

If a phrase were needed to capture the essence of weddings of the 1950s, it would certainly be the "era of novelty." The pages of magazines abounded with pictures featuring unusual designs characteristic of the happy days of the 1950s.

As designers experimented and creativity became one of the most outstanding qualities a bouquet could possess, florists concocted some unusual arrangements. These designs included: butterfly bouquets made of clusters of flowers designed on a wire butterfly form; colonial bouquets in lace bouquet holders; heart bouquets made in the shape of a heart; parasols of satin, lace, or maline outlined in a flower garland; and wedding bells made of stiffened lace incorporated into bouquets.

The bride who wore dotted Swiss was encouraged to carry a bouquet of daisies with a ribbon bow and

c. 1955 This high-fashion bride holding a clutch bouquet of white roses captures the elegance and look of Jacqueline Bouvier Kennedy. **OPPOSITE:** c. 1973 Southern charm flowed in this wedding as the bride displayed a parasol of red and white roses.

matching circlet of daisies to hold her veil. A modern street-length dress of white faille would look stunning with a bouquet of white roses and a matching circlet of small roses in the bride's hair.

Three important society weddings in the 1950s fueled interest in floral designs for weddings: Queen Elizabeth II to Prince Philip in 1947, John F. Kennedy to Jacqueline Lee Bouvier in 1953, and Grace Kelly to Prince Rainier of Monaco in 1956. Brides began to ask for bouquets "like the Queen's." Also in the 1950s, bouquets began to feature tropical flowers such as anthuriums and birds of paradise.

WEDDINGS FOR THE FLOWER CHILD: 1960-1979
Wedding designs in the 1960s began to reflect the social aspects occurring in America, much of which rolled over into the 1970s. Young people began to seek a more organic or back-to-nature approach to their lifestyles.

As the decade progressed, a style all its own began to emerge. Traditional white wedding gowns gave way to caftans and peasant smocks. Many young couples wrote their own vows, challenging or even rejecting the established wedding customs and mores of previous generations. Often, the large white wedding gave way to an intimate gathering as couples opted for alternatives in wedding rituals. Nuptials were performed in parks, on sea cliffs, or overlooking waterfalls high in the mountains. Many such weddings all but curtailed the need for elaborate flowers.

Brides still carried many of the standard bouquet styles but with fewer artificial accessories, particularly in the 1970s. Duchess roses and lilies were still used but with wheat, grapes, peacock feathers, and succulents as natural additions. Baby's breath and daisies became popular, and earth-tone colors were preferred over sprayed gold or silver. Natural-looking hand and arm

bouquets became popular again with accents of ivy garlands or tropical leaves fashioned into loops like ribbons.

Many brides wore flowers in their hair instead of veils. Garlanded hair wreaths and clusters of flowers designed in crescents, ovals, and asymmetrical forms were popular additions worn to the front, side, and back of many young women's hairdos. Small flowers such as daisies or bits of baby's breath were pinned in the hair.

Ethnic diversity was celebrated, and floral designs took their inspiration from the far corners of the world. Included as bridal accents were beads from Africa, coins from Asia, and feathers from Mexico.

PRELUDE TO THE 21ST CENTURY: 1980-1998

When Lady Diana Spencer married Prince Charles, heir to the British throne, large, lavish weddings were once again back in style. Lady Diana's dress was made of yards and yards of white silk taffeta covered with thousands of hand embroidered pearls and beads. Her wedding bouquet was a grand display of romance, not only in design but in actual size, as it nearly grazed the ground.

Inspired by Lady Diana's magnificent bouquet, large cascading bouquets became popular in the early part of the 1980s. These bouquets were constructed of costly flowers and required tedious handwork. Floral designers began turning to Europe for inspiration. They developed designs of structured natural symmetrical or asymmetrical forms and incorporated unusual plant materials. Structured bouquets included vegetative, new convention, pavé, and hand-tied Biedermeier. By the end of the 1980s, American designers were taking the best of design from around the world, incorporating it with what they already knew, and creating their own, more relaxed, "new" American style of bridal work.

In the 1990s, the design phrase that best describes wedding work is "everything old is new again" as brides, in our technology/media-driven world, long for simpler times. Floral designs have taken a softened, romantic, garden-like approach to bridal fashion. Gone are the stiff, structured, Euro-style floral bouquets fashionable in the 1980s.

Like the Victorians a century ago, designers have romanticized history with bridal bouquets that feature charming clusters of opened roses, lilies, garden flowers, and yards of beautiful ribbon. The styles have been updated with new colors and varieties of flowers, but antiquity is celebrated nonetheless.

The marriage of John F. Kennedy Jr. to Carolyn Bessette was a classic 1990s wedding. The private nuptials incorporated the exact mixture to ensure a perfect wedding: a beautiful couple, a romantic setting, guests that included only family and close friends, and pretty flowers. Ms. Bessette's wedding bouquet superbly illustrated the '90s floral style as it was a classic renaissance of the old-fashioned posy or tussie-mussie bouquet.

Wedding bouquet styles that have remained popular or come back into fashion in the 1990s maintain a garden influence and include the shower bouquet, though smaller and more rounded; gentle crescents; tussie-mussies; graceful pointed ovals; and sentimental, classic rounds.

For better or worse, for richer or poorer, in war and peace, bridal floral fashions are constantly reinvented. Like the humble tussie-mussie of yesterday, styles re-emerge over the decades. Flowers, though, will always symbolize love, happiness, and hope, as couples gaze into each others eyes and say, "I DO."

Excerpted from "Weddings," written by Holly Money-Collins, AIFD, for *A Centennial History of the American Florist* © 1997.

OPPOSITE: c. 1981 Lady Diana Spencer carried an elaborate cascading bouquet of roses and stephanotises. AP/WIDE WORLD PHOTOS **BELOW:** c. 1995 The groom sips champagne and balances a bouquet of peonies, delphiniums, bells of Ireland, and spider plants. The bride holds a hand-tied bouquet of delphiniums and soft ribbon.

PHOTO COURTESY OF FLORIST JOAN MERRY

Spring
WEDDINGS

HYACINTH • ROSE • VIBURNUM • TULIP • VERONICA • GINGHAM RIBBON • HYACINTH • ROSE

VIBURNUM • TULIP • VERONICA • GINGHAM RIBBON • HYACINTH • ROSE • VIBURNUM • TULIP

VERONICA • GINGHAM RIBBON • HYACINTH • VIBURNUM • TULIP • VERONICA • GINGHAM

RIBBON • HYACINTH • VIBURNUM • GINGHAM RIBBON • HYACINTH

ROSE • VIBURNUM • ROSE • VIBURNUM

TULIP • VERONICA • GI TULIP • VERONICA

GINGHAM RIBBON • GINGHAM RIBBON

HYACINTH • ROSE ACINTH • ROSE

VIBURNUM • TULIP VIBURNUM • TULIP

VERONICA • GINGHAM ONICA • GINGHAM

RIBBON • HYA HAM RIBBON • HYACINTH

ROSE • VIBURNUM • TULIP • VERON N • ROSE • VIBURNUM

TULIP • VERONICA • GINGHAM RIB LIP • VERONICA • TULIP • VERONICA

GINGHAM RIBBON • HYACINTH • RO LIP • VERONICA • GINGHAM RIBBON

HYACINTH • ROSE • VIBURNUM • T NGHAM RIBBON • HYACINTH • ROSE

VIBURNUM • TULIP • VERONICA • G AM RIB ACINTH • ROSE • VIBURNUM • TULIP

VERONICA • GINGHAM RIBBON • HYACINTH • ROSE • VIBURNUM • TULIP • VERONICA • GINGHAM

RIBBON • HYACINTH • ROSE • VIBURNUM • TULIP • VERONICA • GINGHAM RIBBON • HYACINTH

Bouquets

SET THE MOOD

DANIEL RAY, COURTESY OF ELEGANT BRIDE

DANIEL RAY, COURTESY OF ELEGANT BRIDE

DANIEL RAY, COURTESY OF ELEGANT BRIDE

for SPRING

MARK ROBBINS, COURTESY OF ELEGANT BRIDE

DANIEL RAY, COURTESY OF ELEGANT BRIDE

MARK ROBBINS, COURTESY OF ELEGANT BRIDE

BELOW: Fragrant lilies-of-the-valley gathered in a silver Victorian posy holder are the epitome of today's bouquets–dense, compact, and containing only one specially chosen type of flower.

wedding white

Bouquets of white spring flowers are exquisite in their simplicity. The fluffy white rose and French lilac bouquet (OPPOSITE) softens the crisp tailored lines of the halter-style bridal gown.

Treasured especially for weddings, a lavish profusion of lilies-of-the-valley (ABOVE LEFT, AND BELOW RIGHT) are the consummate bridal bouquet.

Equally attractive, a sweetly scented nosegay bouquet of star-shaped stephanotises (ABOVE RIGHT) makes for a sophisticated choice. To hold the stephanotis blossoms in place, insert the stems of the stephanotis through a cluster of pale green hydrangea. The multiple layers create a lace-like illusion.

DANIEL RAY, COURTESY OF ELEGANT BRIDE

DANIEL RAY, COURTESY OF ELEGANT BRIDE

MARK ROBBINS, COURTESY OF ELEGANT BRIDE

tailored tussies

The dense formality of Biedermeier-style bouquets is the finishing touch to these trimly tailored bridal gowns. A bridesmaid's bouquet (OPPOSITE AND ABOVE LEFT) is created in contrasting pastels beginning with tufts of lavender hydrangeas ringed with a thin row of light pink nerines and finished with respective rows of pale peach roses and foliage.

The bride's bouquet (ABOVE LEFT) is composed of a hand-tied center cluster of hydrangeas surrounded by French lilacs. Its elegant styling is perfect when paired with flowing organza ribbon.

Pale peach roses (ABOVE RIGHT) surround fragrant stems of hyacinth. A second row of hyacinth blooms, threaded into a garland, are cleverly wrapped below the roses.

BELOW: Small, fragrant bouquets are perfectly suited for flower girls and bridesmaids. The oversized organza bow adds a translucent accent perfect for springtime weddings.

DANIEL RAY, COURTESY OF ELEGANT BRIDE

Flowering branches signify the onset of springtime. The unlikely union of winter's branches with a playful scatter of dancing blossoms is a perfect symbol of the new life a wedding heralds for the happy couple.

Showcasing the red-violet hues, this cascading arrangement (OPPOSITE) combines roses, poppies, anemones, muscari, spirea branches, lilacs, and mini callas.

Fragrant lilacs, sweet William, and ivy (ABOVE LEFT) blend to form a richly jeweled clutch.

A graceful bouquet (ABOVE CENTER) of dogwood branches, pink roses, and ivy appears weightless in its delicate presentation.

Fresh pink roses (ABOVE RIGHT) contrast with a garden cutting of lime green viburnum.

DANIEL RAY, COURTESY OF ELEGANT BRIDE

MARK ROBBINS, COURTESY OF ELEGANT BRIDE

tulip time

Considered symbolic of perfect love, tulips were one of the first flowers to be cultivated for their beauty alone. Today they reflect a bride's beauty when carried at springtime ceremonies.

Spectacular double-petaled tulips (OPPOSITE, ABOVE LEFT AND ABOVE RIGHT) are hand-tied into a gardeny cascade bouquet. Slightly open, more mature tulips are essential for this bouquet style.

To create the curved stems, place the tulips diagonally in a container of water so that the midpoint of the stems leans on the container's edge. The flowers will grow outward and down, yielding the cascading components of these bouquets.

Tulips are just as stunning in informal arrangements (ABOVE MIDDLE) and are perfect at receptions or guest book tables.

BELOW: Hand-tied French tulips, detailed with ribbon bindings, are a fresh, easy way to celebrate spring weddings.

MARK ROBBINS, COURTESY OF ELEGANT BRIDE

sun-drenched beauty

The angular cascade bouquets, first popular during the 1930s, are updated here with a loosely gathered hand-tie of tulips and a sleek, modern crescent of callas. Yellow callas and liriope (ABOVE) form a tailored asymmetrical crescent bouquet. Closely grouped double freesias and sprigs of forest green coffee foliage add color and textural contrast without detracting from the boldness of the callas.

Like daffodils against a late winter snow, sunny yellow flowers radiate against the white of a bridal gown. Yellow double tulips (OPPOSITE AND BOTTOM RIGHT) are expertly hand-tied in a cascade of snowblinding brightness.

MARK ROBBINS, COURTESY OF ELEGANT BRIDE

JOE COMICK, COURTESY OF ELEGANT BRIDE

JOE COMICK, COURTESY OF ELEGANT BRIDE

JOE COMICK, COURTESY OF ELEGANT BRIDE

MARK ROBBINS, COURTESY OF ELEGANT BRIDE

spring harvest

Enjoying a lovely day for a garden wedding, these lilac-clad bridesmaids (OPPOSITE), each wearing a different style of dress, are carrying a quick-to-create "sheaf" bouquet. The versatile and stylish bouquets of larkspur and false spirea are casually held in the arms or gracefully inverted toward the ground.

A berry-colored gathering basket (ABOVE), tied with gingham streamers and filled to overflowing, is a substantial accent. The basket may be carried as a bouquet and later placed as a table centerpiece.

The bride (ABOVE RIGHT) looks radiant with her "something blue" arm bouquet of delphinium and larkspur, designed to complement the vivid brides-maids' dresses. Her delicate halo of elaeagnus leaves and larkspur echo the appliqué on her organza gown.

"Sheaf" bouquets allow each attendant to carry her bouquet in the manner most comfortable to her and best suited to her gown.

French lilacs and blush-colored roses form a fresh-picked garden bouquet cascading with strands of variegated English ivy (also shown opposite lower right).

DANIEL RAY, COURTESY OF ELEGANT BRIDE

MARK ROBBINS, COURTESY OF ELEGANT BRIDE

blushing bouquets

Traditionalists insist on the bride carrying all white flowers while the modernists opt for vivid color. A happy medium might be these delicately hued bouquets blushed with the lightest touch of pink and peach. Coffee foliage frames bouvardia, lilies, tulips, freesias, and roses (ABOVE LEFT) in shades from antique white to pink. They tumble from the bouquet holder in an unconstructed cascade, as if gathered by hand from a Victorian garden.

A simple nosegay (ABOVE TOP) of tightly massed, peach-colored French tulips is trimmed with a broad sheer ribbon with woven satin edges. The hue of the ribbon has been perfected with a light dusting of spray paint.

FAR RIGHT AND ABOVE: A bridesmaid's delicate nosegay of violets sets the stage for the wedding floral theme, which is enhanced with coordinating boutonnieres, a welcoming wreath **(ABOVE)**, and even a purse adornment for mother **(BELOW)**, all fashioned of dewy fresh sweet violets.

The mention of sweet violets conjures up romantic memories of a bygone age of innocence and old-fashioned beauty. Today, California-grown violets are still available from mid-November to mid-April, adding a nostalgic detail to a springtime ceremony.

The quiet beauty of violets, accented with their own deep green foliage, seems most attractive against simple, solid-colored dresses. Yet they are also perfect when paired with the most fussy of Victorian laces. Whatever the case, violets are too fragile to survive overhandling and the trauma of being mixed with other flowers, so a small nosegay tied with organza ribbon is often best.

To re-create the sweet violet nosegay when they are out of season, try surrounding millinery-quality, velvet violets with a fresh collar of galax or cyclamen leaves.

Violet stems can remain exposed for a fresh picked appearance.

DOGWOOD • PANSEY • ZINNIA • QUEEN ANNE'S LACE • ASPARAGUS FERN • DOGWOOD • PANSEY

ZINNIA • QUEEN ANNE'S LACE • ASPARAGUS FERN • DOGWOOD • PANSEY • ZINNIA • QUEEN

ANNE'S LACE • ASPARAGUS FERN • DOGWOOD • QUEEN ANNE'S LACEASPARAGUS

FERN • DOGWOOD • PAN ASPARAGUS FERN • DOGWOOD

PANSEY • ZINNIA • QUEEN WOOD PANSEY • ZINNIA

QUEEN ANNE'S LACE QUEEN ANNE'S LACE

ASPARAGUS FERN CE ASPARAGUS FERN

DOGWOOD • PANSEY • DOGWOOD • PANSEY

ZINNIA • QUEEN AN SEY ZINNIA • QUEEN

ANNE'S LACE • ASPAR QUEEN ANNE'S LACE

ASPARAGUS FERN • D CE • ASPARAGUS FERN

DOGWOOD • PANSEY S FERN • DOGWOOD • PANSEY

ZINNIA • QUEEN ANNE'S LA OD • PANSEY • ZINNIA • QUEEN

ANNE'S LACE • ASPARAGUS ZINNIA • QUEEN ANNE'S LACE

ASPARAGUS FERN • DOGWOOD EN ANNE'S LACE • ASPARAGUS FERN-

DOGWOOD • PANSEY • ZINNIA • QUEE LACE • ASPARAGUS FERN • DOGWOOD • PANSEY

ZINNIA • QUEEN ANNE'S LACE • ASPARAGUS FERN • DOGWOOD • PANSEY • ZINNIA • QUEEN

ANNE'S LACE • ASPARAGUS FERN • DOGWOOD • PANSEY • ZINNIA • QUEEN ANNE'S

pretty pansies

The French believed that pansies could make your lover think of you and the Celts made a love potion tea from the pansies' leaves, but today it's best to remember the vibrant annual as a colorful flower for weddings.

Pansies, asters, zinnias, Queen Anne's lace, and dogwood blossoms (OPPOSITE), all air-dried to perfection for an ever-lasting option, compose this cascade bouquet.

Freshly picked purple pansies (ABOVE) are set on an antique lace handkerchief–a delicate keepsake for generations to cherish.

Pansies give flavor to the party (RIGHT) when defining the border of a cake table and garnishing a plate for the always-present wedding mints.

JOE COMICK, COURTESY OF ELEGANT BRIDE

JOE COMICK, COURTESY OF ELEGANT BRIDE

ABOVE: The relaxed formality of this tightly massed nosegay of creamy tulips, freesias, and grape hyacinths makes a faultless choice for the simple lines of tailored suits.

IMMEDIATE LEFT: The mother of the bride carries a nosegay of love-in-a-mist, elaeagnus, and delphinium blossoms.

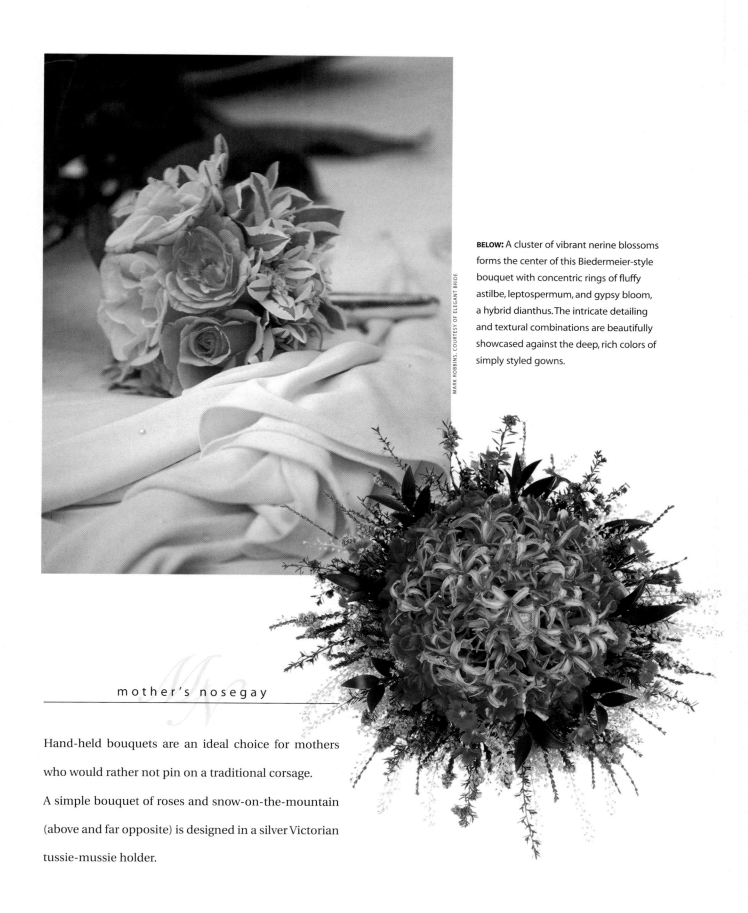

MARK ROBBINS, COURTESY OF ELEGANT BRIDE

BELOW: A cluster of vibrant nerine blossoms forms the center of this Biedermeier-style bouquet with concentric rings of fluffy astilbe, leptospermum, and gypsy bloom, a hybrid dianthus. The intricate detailing and textural combinations are beautifully showcased against the deep, rich colors of simply styled gowns.

mother's nosegay

Hand-held bouquets are an ideal choice for mothers who would rather not pin on a traditional corsage. A simple bouquet of roses and snow-on-the-mountain (above and far opposite) is designed in a silver Victorian tussie-mussie holder.

Boutonnieres

A D D   D I S T I N C T I O N

Originally, a boutonniere was a single blossom taken from the bride's bouquet during the wedding ceremony and slipped through a buttonhole on the lapel of the groom's jacket. Modern boutonnieres, usually pinned to the lapel, add distinction to today's well-dressed grooms and their men.

A popular springtime option, individual rose petals (1)

rolled with one encircling another, gives a different dimension to the most favorite boutonniere flower.

Diminutive violets (2) are combined with bold variegated euonymus to form a modern, classic boutonniere.

Variegated and green ivy leaves, (3) symbols of marital fidelity, are fashioned into an affordable but elegant foliage boutonniere.

ABOVE: Exotic dendrobium orchids, barely blushing with color, make a grand statement in this simple styling, absent of foliage

OPPOSITE: Delphinium florets and individual bells of Ireland combine for a fleet of buttonhole beauties.

A fragrant exotic "fantasy" flower (4) is created by threading single hyacinth blossoms consecutively onto a length of wire inserted into the top floret.

Delphinium florets (5), clustered into a miniature composite flower, create a novel boutonniere.

for S P R I N G

Celebration

S E T T I N G S

JOE COMICK, COURTESY OF ELEGANT BRIDE

MARK ROBBINS, COURTESY OF ELEGANT BRIDE

JOE COMICK, COURTESY OF ELEGANT BRIDE

in S P R I N G

MARK ROBBINS, COURTESY OF ELEGANT BRIDE

spring confections

The wedding cake (ABOVE) becomes the centerpiece of an elegantly appointed table when enhanced with a vibrantly colored collection of fresh fragrant blossoms. The bouquets of the bride and her attendants are placed nearby for additional decoration.

Bridesmaids' bouquets (OPPOSITE AND RIGHT) are composed of soft lavender and peach-colored roses and stock. The compact design makes a light-weight and fragrant bouquet that shimmers in the soft glow of spring.

JOE COMICK, COURTESY OF ELEGANT BRIDE

MARK ROBBINS, COURTESY OF ELEGANT BRIDE

MARK ROBBINS, COURTESY OF ELEGANT BRIDE

MARK ROBBINS, COURTESY OF ELEGANT BRIDE

vivid veranda

This stunning veranda illustrates how the careful coordination of floral arrangements and linens can heighten the impact of a celebration. Transforming the outdoors into a formal reception, the summery colors of the flowers are repeated in the patterned table skirts, which are topped with a solid lavender overcloth. Coordinating flowers adorn the chair coverings and cake top. Flowers are prominent in every available and appropriate space.

ABOVE TOP: A delicate nosegay of lavender larkspur florets decorates the cake top in faux-violet fashion.

ABOVE BOTTOM: Two colors of stock and a single rose are slipped into the chair's bow for an extra special detail.

MARK ROBBINS, COURTESY OF ELEGANT BRIDE

evening nuptials

The bridal party (OPPOSITE) is surrounded by a flurry of flowers. Larkspur, delphiniums, and bells-of-Ireland encompass the altar, creating a glorious backdrop for the ceremony. A candle-bearing arrangement with larkspur, delphinium, bells-of-Ireland, elaeagnus, and salal is placed beside each pew. Fresh wreaths (ABOVE) of coordinating flowers and foliage are hung on the chapel doors to warmly welcome guests. The wreath begins with a weaving of sturdy ivy strands to which salal leaves, delphinium florets, stock, and dahlia blossoms are added.

MARK ROBBINS, COURTESY OF ELEGANT BRIDE

ABOVE: Entry to the chapel is a detail not to be overlooked. A frame of southern smilax and elaeagnus around the chapel doors creates an intimate romantic wedding fantasy in a forgotten country chapel. To create a similar ambiance at other wedding locations, weave foliage cuttings loosely around the entryway architecture.

LEFT AND OPPOSITE TOP CENTER: A pensive flower girl holds a spring green floral pomander fashioned from the individual florets of bells-of-Ireland.

JOE COMICK, COURTESY OF ELEGANT BRIDE

MARK ROBBINS, COURTESY OF ELEGANT BRIDE

MARK ROBBINS, COURTESY OF ELEGANT BRIDE

MARK ROBBINS, COURTESY OF ELEGANT BRIDE

distinctive details

Limiting flowers and foliage to a few varieties repeated throughout a wedding can enhance the overall scheme. These flowers become predominant elements used in the bouquets, alter pieces and pew decorations. They also create a framework or theme for the wedding environment. In this setting, the bridal bouquet, alter pieces and pew decorations are comprised primarily of delphiniums, larkspur, and bells-of-Ireland and limited to the colors of white, blue and green.

The bouquets (TOP LEFT AND RIGHT) are monochromatic, free-style collections of larkspur, delphiniums, roses, and bells-of-Ireland, tied with a touch of gingham ribbon. Arrangements are kept fresh in simple containers of water.

A candle-bearing clay pot (BOTTOM RIGHT) containing larkspur, delphinium, bells-of-Ireland, Elaeagnus, and salal is placed beside each pew.

MARK ROBBINS, COURTESY OF ELEGANT BRIDE

MARK ROBBINS, COURTESY OF ELEGANT BRIDE

MARK ROBBINS, COURTESY OF ELEGANT BRIDE

garden party

For weddings in spring, few things are more elegant and sophisticated than all white florals with a traditional touch of blue. An abundant composition of white tulips (OPPOSITE AND RIGHT) has a particularly distinctive impact with all the blossoms placed on the same level.

An ivy garland (OPPOSITE) softens the silver saucer, and silver "vases" of dainty grape hyacinths serve as favors for guests.

Ivy leaf placemats (ABOVE LEFT) add the finishing touch to table settings. To make the placemats, use a spray adhesive to attach overlapping ivy leaves to kraft paper. Mats are then sprayed with a glossy sealant, stored between wax paper, and pressed flat under a weight to prevent curling.

ABOVE: Bulb flowers herald the arrival of spring like no others, and simple compositions often showcase them to their fullest.

MARK ROBBINS, COURTESY OF ELEGANT BRIDE

Summer

W E D D I N G S

ROSE • RANUNCULUS • BOUVARDIA • DAISY CHRYSANTHEMUM • SALAL FOLIAGE • DAISY

POMPON • ROSE • RANUNCULUS • BOUVARDIA • DAISY CHRYSANTHEMUM • SALAL FOLIAGE

DAISY POMPON • ROSE • RANUNCULUS • BOUVARDIA • DAISY CHRYSANTHEMUM • SALAL FOLIAGE

ROSE • RANUNCULUS • BOUVARDIA • DAISY CHRYSANTHEMUM • SALAL FOLIAGE • DAISY POMPON

RANUNCULUS • BOUVARDIA • DAISY CHRYSANTHEMUM • SALAL FOLIAGE • DAISY POMPON • ROSE

BOUVARDIA • DAISY CHRYSANTHEMUM • SALAL FOLIAGE • DAISY POMPON • ROSE • RANUNCULUS

DAISY CHRYSANTHEMUM • SALAL FOLIAGE • DAISY POMPON • ROSE • RANUNCULUS • BOUVARDIA

SALAL FOLIAGE • DAISY POMPON • ROSE • RANUNCULUS • BOUVARDIA • DAISY CHRYSANTHEMUM

DAISY POMPON • ROSE • RANUNCULUS • BOUVARDIA • DAISY CHRYSANTHEMUM • SALAL FOLIAGE

ROSE • RANUNCULUS • BOUVARDIA • DAISY CHRYSANTHEMUM • SALAL FOLIAGE • DAISY POMPON

SALAL FOLIAGE • DAISY POMPON • ROSE • RANUNCULUS • BOUVARDIA • DAISY CHRYSANTHEMUM

DAISY POMPON • ROSE • RANUNCULUS • BOUVARDIA • DAISY CHRYSANTHEMUM • SALAL FOLIAGE

Bouquets

SET THE MOOD

JOE COMICK, COURTESY OF ELEGANT BRIDE

MARK ROBBINS, COURTESY OF ELEGANT BRIDE

JOE COMICK, COURTESY OF ELEGANT BRIDE

for SUMMER

MARK ROBBINS, COURTESY OF ELEGANT BRIDE

MARK ROBBINS, COURTESY OF ELEGANT BRIDE

rose romance

The glorious rose has been the sentimental flower of choice for brides for many years. Our multi-variety bouquets embody the nostalgia of grandmother's cutting garden including everything from hybrid teas to clustered floribundas. In creating these classic round bouquets, blended colors of roses in varying states of openness were chosen to coordinate with the softly colored bridesmaids' dresses. To add a fresh summer look for the bride's bouquet (OPPOSITE), delicate wisps of grass-green tulle were added to the bouquet, softly setting it apart from her gown.

A bouquet of roses and snow-on-the-mountain (ABOVE LEFT) is designed in a silver Victorian tussie-mussie holder.

A berry-colored gathering basket (ABOVE RIGHT) overflows with an assortment of violet-hued blossoms including, of course, the legendary rose.

BELOW: Small nosegays of soft multicolored roses coordinate with the individually styled gowns of bridesmaids.

MARK ROBBINS, COURTESY OF ELEGANT BRIDE

MARK ROBBINS, COURTESY OF ELEGANT BRIDE

cymbidium orchids

MARK ROBBINS, COURTESY OF ELEGANT BRIDE

MARK ROBBINS, COURTESY OF ELEGANT BRIDE

The affordable cymbidium orchid's delicate beauty, hardy nature, and year-round availability makes it one of the most sought-after and reliable bridal choices. The opaque coloring of white cymbidiums (ABOVE) lends a "floating" appearance, while an elongated shape makes this bouquet a perfect choice for a traditional celebration.

Pink cymbidium orchids, carnations, and lavender field asters (BELOW RIGHT) overflow from an antique reproduction posy holder. The simplicity of this arrangement makes it particularly appropriate for a second wedding.

MARK ROBBINS, COURTESY OF ELEGANT BRIDE

JOE COMICK, COURTESY OF ELEGANT BRIDE

garden menagerie

The variety of colors and forms in these bouquets enrich their appearance.

Nature's own botanical bounty is as assorted as it is facinating. With all the different choices available during any particular season, how can one decide? Maybe the choice is to include one of everything. With each bloom chosen for its unique beauty, these multicolored summer nosegays (OPPOSITE AND RIGHT) of roses, lisianthuses, panicle hydrangeas, and zinnias showcase a medley of garden diversity. Two streamers of wide mocha-colored ribbon, a contemporary neutral, accent the bouquets and dresses with an unexpected hue.

Three tussie-mussie-styled bouquets (ABOVE), each with a rose variety of their own, are designed in silver Victorian bouquet holders.

MARK ROBBINS, COURTESY OF ELEGANT BRIDE

ORIENTAL STARGAZER LILY • ORIENTAL STARGAZER LILY • ORIENTAL STARGAZER LILY • ORIENTAL
STARGAZER LILY • ORIENTAL STARGAZER LILY • ORIENTAL STARGAZER LILY • ORIENTAL STARGAZER
LILY • ORIENTAL STARGAZER LILY • ORIENTAL STARGAZER LILY • ORIENTAL STARGAZER LILY
ORIENTAL STARGAZER LILY • ORIENTAL STARGAZER LILY • ORIENTAL STARGAZER LILY • ORIENTAL
STARGAZER LILY • ORIENTAL STARGAZER LILY • ORIENTAL STARGAZER LILY • ORIENTAL STARGAZER
LILY • ORIENTAL STARGAZER LILY • ORIENTAL STARGAZER LILY • ORIENTAL STARGAZER LILY
ORIENTAL STARGAZER LILY • ORIENTAL STARGAZER LILY • ORIENTAL STARGAZER LILY • ORIENTAL
STARGAZER LILY • ORIENTAL STARGAZER LILY • ORIENTAL STARGAZER LILY • ORIENTAL STARGAZER
LILY • ORIENTAL STARGAZER LILY • ORIENTAL STARGAZER LILY • ORIENTAL STARGAZER LILY
ORIENTAL STARGAZER LILY • ORIENTAL STARGAZER LILY • ORIENTAL STARGAZER LILY • ORIENTAL
STARGAZER LILY • ORIENTAL STARGAZER LILY • ORIENTAL STARGAZER LILY • ORIENTAL STARGAZER
LILY • ORIENTAL STARGAZER LILY • ORIENTAL STARGAZER LILY • ORIENTAL STARGAZER LILY •
ORIENTAL STARGAZER LILY • ORIENTAL STARGAZER LILY • ORIENTAL STARGAZER LILY • ORIENTAL
STARGAZER LILY • ORIENTAL STARGAZER LILY • ORIENTAL STARGAZER LILY • ORIENTAL STARGAZER
LILY • ORIENTAL STARGAZER LILY • ORIENTAL STARGAZER LILY • ORIENTAL STARGAZER LILY
ORIENTAL STARGAZER LILY • ORIENTAL STARGAZER LILY • ORIENTAL STARGAZER LILY • ORIENTAL
STARGAZER LILY • ORIENTAL STARGAZER LILY • ORIENTAL STARGAZER LILY • ORIENTAL STARGAZER
LILY • ORIENTAL STARGAZER LILY • ORIENTAL STARGAZER LILY • ORIENTAL STARGAZER LILY

oriental lilies

With a simple geometry of form that's almost architectural, these bold, angular blossoms command attention whether massed in a luscious bouquet or quietly blooming on the plant. In the language of flowers, lilies symbolize renewed life. This is because of the ability of the flowers to bloom even after the foliage has died, as well as their ability to simultaneously sustain flowers from tiny green buds to proudly unfurled trumpets.

The simple formality of this Oriental lily cascade (OPPOSITE) is perfectly suited to simple, formal dresses.

An asymmetrical, contemporary look (ABOVE LEFT) incorporates the darkest of pink blossoms, lily foliage, and eucalyptus, plus loops of liriope fronds.

ABOVE: The elaborate composite lily bouquet starts with a single lily in the center. Individual petals are wired and taped in place, expanding the blossom. The bouquet's tight formation helps the petals retain their shape longer, since the lily is prone to fast wilting without a water source.

fragrant hearts

BELOW: Rows of delphinium, miniature carnations and sweetheart roses, with a heather center, forms an extra special cake top. To create the ruffled ribbon base, simply pull the wire along one side of a length of French-wired ribbon.

Recognized worldwide as the icon of love, the heart, shaped here from roses, is the perfect wedding symbol, communicating a shapely message in flowers.

A delicious pavé centerpiece (OPPOSITE) of peach and pink roses, tailored with an edge of rosebuds, is formed in a heart-shaped cake pan to match the attendants' rose bouquets.

Spray roses (ABOVE RIGHT), wired and taped to form a heart shape, are bundled with ribbon embroidered with delicate rosebuds.

Two pink-edged 'Anna' roses, as well as pink astible and gold bullion (ABOVE), are featured within a heart-shaped frame wrapped with gold metallic ribbon.

The terms tussie-mussie, posy, and nosegay are used interchangeably when referring to a small round bouquet of flowers that are hand-held or attached to clothing. Originally, however, tussie was a medieval word meaning a knot of flowers, and mussie referred to a clump of moist moss that kept the flowers fresh. Posy was once the poem that accompanied the bouquet, and nosegay refered to the fragrant flowers and herbs that, when held to the nose, was believed to not only relieve the stench associated with medieval life but also to ward off disease.

Hybrid tea roses, butterfly asters, monkshood, agapanthus, and a dusting of limonium fill an urn to overflowing. At its base is a complementary nosegay, composed of the same flower varieties, accented with a sheer wire-edged ribbon of deep blue.

nosegay bouquets

These four bouquets demonstrate the international influence that contributed to the formation of what we generally refer to today as nosegays. A French nosegay (1) of delphiniums, statice, freesias, and roses, tucked with tufts of organza ribbon, was considered a status symbol of the carriage society. The American colonial (2), a sweet harmony of strictly seasonal and indiginous blossoms such as irises, daisies, roses, and 'Monte Cassino' asters, reflects the limitations of the pioneering lifestyle. An English garden posy (3) filled with anemones, dianthuses, nerines, freesias, tulips, heather, and statice represents the Victorian floral code in which every flower and foliage choice carried with it a special message. Finally, a German Biedermeier-style nosegay (4) made of tulips, roses, statice, nerines, and heather exhibits the design's trademark concentric circles.

DANIEL RAY, COURTESY OF ELEGANT BRIDE

MARK ROBBINS, COURTESY OF ELEGANT BRIDE

LEFT, ABOVE, AND TOP OPPOSITE:
Glowing with vivid color against a
white bridal gown, this arrangement
of orange Scarborough lilies, yellow
Ornithogalum, parrot tulips, and
red berries emanates the fiery
warmth of summer.

DANIEL RAY, COURTESY OF ELEGANT BRIDE

vivid brights

Since the turn of the century, white flowers were a bridal standard. But today, bright flowers reflect the confidence and surety of a self-determined bride while imparting a thoroughly modern sense of style.

Celosia, multicolored zinnias, and stock (LEFT) are detailed with a touch of orange ribbon for a colonial-style bridesmaid's accessory.

1 **2**

3 **4**

5 **6**

LON MURDICK, COURTESY OF ELEGANT BRIDE

1. Roses, in three different hues of pink and three shades of creamy white, compose a dainty silver-ribboned nosegay.

2. Six lavender sweetheart roses are framed with rose leaves and 'Misty Blue' limonium.

3. Single-stemmed Chinese miniature carnations are tucked in silver-enhanced salal leaves.

4. Nerine blossoms and sprigs of leptospermum peek out from a gathering of ornamental ferns.

5. An herby Biedermeier-style bouquet is composed of rosemary, heather, and roses tied with a watercolor-washed organza ribbon.

6. Daisy poms arranged in a pavé formation lay in a bed of bunched tulle and ribbon.

sentimental nosegays

The wedding ensemble is never complete without the perfect florals. These options show variations on a theme. This casual concentric colonial (ABOVE) is a stately combination of anemones, lisianthuses, and lilies fringed with a collar of pink and white larkspur and finished with damask ribbon.

Boutonnieres

ADD DISTINCTION

Just as important as the bride's and bridesmaids' flowers, boutonnieres should not be treated as small details that will go unnoticed. Buttonhole flowers are essential accouterments of men's special occasion attire, and they too should be crafted with the utmost of care so that the boutonniere-clad groom feels as distinguished and handsome as his bride feels elegant and beautiful.

Brightly colored kaffir lilies (1), each with a carefully taped stem, are delightful selections for summertime weddings with vibrant color themes.

Distinguish the groom and his groomsmen (2) with a single miniature calla blossom, accented by seeded eucalyptus or short sprigs of foliage.

The trio of white freesias (3), enhanced by buds and banded with decorative gold wire, makes a chic and handsome boutonniere as well.

The favorite, however, remains the venerable rose boutonniere (4) for both groom and groomsmen.

MARK ROBBINS, COURTESY OF ELEGANT BRIDE

for SUMMER

Celebration

SETTINGS

JOE COMICK, COURTESY OF ELEGANT BRIDE

MARK ROBBINS, COURTESY OF ELEGANT BRIDE

JOE COMICK, COURTESY OF ELEGANT BRIDE

in SUMMER

JOE COMICK, COURTESY OF ELEGANT BRIDE

MARK ROBBINS, COURTESY OF ELEGANT BRIDE

ABOVE AND RIGHT: Spectacular duchess roses, created with clusters of individual petals, serve as grand bouquets for both the bride to carry and to place on top of the wedding cake.

wedding alfresco

At casually elegant outdoor receptions, centerpieces consisting of terra-cotta containers with gardeny flowers, petals, fruits, and berries add grace to tables. Impact comes from the contrast of columnar topiaries of larkspur, (OPPOSITE) mounded pots of berries, and vibrant mixed blossoms arranged in clustered groups.

RIGHT: Baskets of delicate rose petals stand ready to be showered on the bridal party as they depart.

MARK ROBBINS, COURTESY OF ELEGANT BRIDE

A wreath of elaeagnus and florets of larkspur encircle the bride's hair, taking the place of the traditional veil.

MARK ROBBINS, COURTESY OF ELEGANT BRIDE

MARK ROBBINS, COURTESY OF ELEGANT BRIDE

outdoor elegance

The easy living of summertime is reflected in the most joyful of celebrations – a June wedding.

Careful planning and summer's abundance of fresh available flowers call for careful attention to floral accents. Simple chair treatments (ABOVE RIGHT) of ribbons and cosmos are perfect additions to these well-appointed tables. Ivy, 'Henry Matisse' roses, lavender roses, cosmos, and astilbe (BELOW RIGHT) highlight a collection of assorted summer blossoms in this basket arrangement.

MARK ROBBINS, COURTESY OF ELEGANT BRIDE

MARK ROBBINS, COURTESY OF ELEGANT BRIDE

MARK ROBBINS, COURTESY OF ELEGANT BRIDE

garden grandeur

Few of nature's offerings are more spectacular for summer celebrations than gloriously fragrant Oriental lilies. Here, in hues ranging from soft and delicate to bold and bright, a gardeny profusion of the star-shaped beauties (OPPOSITE) overflow and encircle (in a wet foam wreath ring) an elegant basket-weave terra-cotta pot.

Along with a floral-patterned tablecloth, smaller terra-cotta vessels filled with either flowering kale "rosettes" or nests with robin's eggs enhance the "summer garden" feeling.

The faux lime-and-salt-deposit finish, which gives the pots an aged character, is created with water and flat white spray paint–spraying first with water, then immediately with white paint, and then again with water.

ABOVE LEFT: Satellite pots of flowering kale and potted bird's nests filled with candy eggs make unique favors.

Grapes dipped in egg white and sprinkled with sugar are a glistening confection.

Layer grapes around a champagne bottle in a straight-sided pitcher, fill with water and freeze to create this dramatic ice bucket.

ABOVE: Detailing the legs with stalks of bear grass transforms an ordinary glass-top patio table into a unique reception or cake station.

grape arbor

Decorating the cake with an ordinary bride and goom figurine pales in comparison to this deftly executed decoration of frosted grapes and roses.

Green grapes add a lush and distinctively summer touch to reception settings. A wildly romantic arbor (OPPOSITE) is created with grape ivy foliage, natural branches, and fresh grapes. Let the champagne flow (ABOVE LEFT) in a frozen grape ice bucket.

A double-tiered basket weave cake (ABOVE RIGHT) is deliciously adorned with a fresh combination of grapes, roses, and anemones.

Fall

WEDDINGS

MINIATURE PUMPKIN • MINIATURE SUNFLOWER • GOLDENROD • SQUIRREL TAIL GRASS SATIN

MOIRE RIBBON • PEACH ROSE • MINIATURE PUMPKIN • MINIATURE SUNFLOWER • GOLDENROD

SQUIRREL TAIL GRASS • SATIN MOIRE RIBBON • PEACH ROSE • MINIATURE PUMPKIN

MINIATURE SUNFLOWER • GOLDENROD • SQUIRREL TAIL GRASS • SATIN MOIRE RIBBON

PEACH ROSE • MINIATURE PUMPKIN • MINIATURE SUNFLOWER • GOLDENROD • SQUIRREL TAIL

GRASS • SATIN MOIRE RIBBON • PEACH ROSE • MINIATURE SUNFLOWER

GOLDENROD • SQUIRREL TAIL GRASS • SATIN MOIRE RIBBON • MINIATURE

PUMPKIN • MINIATURE SUNFLOWER • GOLDENROD • SQUIRREL TAIL GRASS • SATIN MOIRE

RIBBON • PEACH ROSE • MINIATURE PUMPKIN • MINIATURE SUNFLOWER • GOLDENROD

SQUIRREL TAIL GRASS • SATIN MOIRE RIBBON • PEACH ROSE • MINIATURE PUMPKIN

MINIATURE SUNFLOWER • GOLDENROD • SQUIRREL TAIL GRASS • SATIN MOIRE RIBBON

PEACH ROSE • MINIATURE PUMPKIN • MINIATURE SUNFLOWER • GOLDENROD • SQUIRREL TAIL

GRASS • SATIN MOIRE RIBBON • PEACH ROSE • MINIATURE SUNFLOWER

GOLDENROD • SQUIRREL TAIL GRASS • SATIN MOIRE RIBBON • PEACH ROSE • MINIATURE

PUMPKIN • MINIATURE SUNFLOWER • GOLDENROD • SQUIRREL TAIL GRASS • SATIN MOIRE

RIBBON • PEACH ROSE • MINIATURE PUMPKIN • MINIATURE SUNFLOWER • GOLDENROD

SQUIRREL TAIL GRASS • SATIN MOIRE RIBBON • PEACH ROSE • MINIATURE PUMPKIN

MINIATURE SUNFLOWER • GOLDENROD • SQUIRREL TAIL GRASS • SATIN MOIRE RIBBON

Bouquets
SET THE MOOD

DANIEL RAY, COURTESY OF ELEGANT BRIDE

DANIEL RAY, COURTESY OF ELEGANT BRIDE

DANIEL RAY, COURTESY OF ELEGANT BRIDE

for FALL

MARK ROBBINS, COURTESY OF ELEGANT BRIDE

simple *s*tarflowers

The scaled-down country look of drieds is enjoying a resurgence in popularity and can be perfect for autumn weddings. A bountiful cluster of starflowers (OPPOSITE AND RIGHT) celebrates the simple aesthetic in American Shaker style. After the ceremony, it becomes a beautiful keepsake. The hand-tied ivory starflowers are wrapped in a lush satin-edged moiré ribbon.

Similarly, fresh and dried flowers can be combined with stunning results. A Biedermeier-inspired bouquet (ABOVE RIGHT) is centered with a cluster of starflowers, ringed with ivory roses, and fringed with foliage.

RIGHT: Everlasting bouquets are ready-made for keepsakes.

MARK ROBBINS, COURTESY OF ELEGANT BRIDE

MARK ROBBINS, COURTESY OF ELEGANT BRIDE

ABOVE: The lovely scent of freesias speaks of sweet romance.

fragrant freesias

For many brides, the fragrance is just as important as the color or shape of the bouquet. The perfumed freesia blossom will bring back warm memories long after photos have faded. Native to South Africa, this delicate bulb flower is available year-round in shades of white, yellow, pink, and violet.

The long stems of a mass of white freesias (OPPOSITE AND ABOVE RIGHT) are gathered and banded with silver beading wire. The bouquet is fringed with foxtail millet for a hint of fall.

A complex scent is achieved by pairing sweet-smelling stephanotises and freesias with bouvardia (ABOVE LEFT). An olive, suede-like bow completes the autumn ensemble.

DANIEL RAY, COURTESY OF ELEGANT BRIDE

MARK ROBBINS, COURTESY OF ELEGANT BRIDE

LEFT: Beading adds unexpected sparkle to floral displays and accents the roses as they gently open throughout the day.

honey tweeds

Like a mixture of contrasting yarns in a finely woven tweed, a carefully chosen mixture of fall-toned florals can yield a bouquet rich in visual textures.

Yellow double freesias, blush roses, amber leucadendron, and mahogany hypericum berries (OPPOSITE AND ABOVE) dance in a nosegay trimmed with sparkling strands of beads.

The rusty brown and parchment gold of the bicolored 'Leonidas' rose (ABOVE LEFT) updates the traditional rose bouquet to a sophisticated tapestry of fall color.

DANIEL RAY, COURTESY OF ELEGANT BRIDE

MARK ROBBINS, COURTESY OF ELEGANT BRIDE

ABOVE: Limber branches woven across the nosegay surface add textural interest.

DANIEL RAY, COURTESY OF ELEGANT BRIDE

ABOVE: The lightweight quality of dusty miller is especially suited to gowns of flowing lace.

fall clutches

Not all bouquets for fall weddings need to be in warm ambered tones. The cool faded blues of dusty miller and the rich lacquered hues of privet, hypericum, and ivy berries make an equally appropriate autumn choice.

Blush roses with a collar of dusty miller (OPPOSITE AND BELOW RIGHT) contrast with a warm camel ribbon for a fall note.

Dusty miller, *Muscari*, lisianthuses, privet berries, and branches (ABOVE LEFT) give a tweedy feel to this fall bouquet.

MARK ROBBINS, COURTESY OF ELEGANT BRIDE

DANIEL RAY, COURTESY OF ELEGANT BRIDE

LEFT: To give standard roses the rambling rose look, pluck the center petals out of a fully open blossom.

Indian summer

Fall bridal bouquets overflow with the colors of turning leaves for splendid autumn accents. Mix gold and amber blossoms with the burgundy and aubergine berries of hypericum and privet.

Cream callas with red-tipped throats (OPPOSITE AND BOTTOM RIGHT) star in this bouquet with exotic leucadendrons, berries, and brilliant orange Scarborough lilies.

A lovely fall bouquet (ABOVE) consists of the warm gold tones of yarrow combined with camellia foliage and yellow roses in a posy holder. Tufts of blue hydrangea are included for a cool-colored contrast.

MARK ROBBINS, COURTESY OF ELEGANT BRIDE

DANIEL RAY, COURTESY OF ELEGANT BRIDE

MARK ROBBINS, COURTESY OF ELEGANT BRIDE

MARK ROBBINS, COURTESY OF ELEGANT BRIDE

DANIEL RAY, COURTESY OF ELEGANT BRIDE

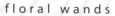

floral wands

Sleek, cocktail-style dresses are a stunning background for the formal simplicity of wand bouquets. Complementary or contrasting bands descend the length of the flower stem or grain stalk, providing both a mechanical and decorative binding.

Supple tangerine callas (OPPOSITE AND ABOVE) are banded with silver beading wire, repeating the slender flowing lines of this dark floral gown. Fresh flower wand bouquets may be delivered in a vase of water, keeping them fresh until ceremony time.

Italian black-bearded wheat wands (RIGHT) make warm, textured bouquets. Drieds are a carefree and elegant fall choice as well as a lasting keepsake.

MARK ROBBINS, COURTESY OF ELEGANT BRIDE

LEFT: Fall bouquets of warm yellows to rusty reds are perfect when carried against dark colors like brown, navy, or black

sunset shades

Blossoms in brilliant autumn colors that reflect the intensity of a desert sunset are best displayed with minimal foliage. Hand-tying gloriosa lilies, miniature callas, and Iceland poppies (OPPOSITE AND ABOVE) into a free-form bouquet–a beautiful palette against almost any of today's rich dress colors–achieves a glorious analogous color harmony.

Pincushion proteas, *Asclepias*, bouvardias, *Gomphrenas*, and freesias (BOTTOM RIGHT) look wonderful when punctuated with glossy salal leaves and vibrant sheer ribbons.

OPPOSITE AND RIGHT: An organza ribbon picks up the crimson markings on the throat of the cymbidium orchid, which looks stunning when paired with a persimmon-colored dress.

MARK ROBBINS, COURTESY OF ELEGANT BRIDE

cymbidium sprays

An elongated pomander bouquet of chartreuse green cymbidium orchids is a contemporary and sturdy bouquet style for today's bride.

Construction of pomanders begins with the wiring and taping of each individual blossom onto florists' wire. They are then assembled starting at the bottom, with each flower placed as close together as possible. A loop of ribbon forms the handle.

Faux Flowers

FOR FALL

Fabric flowers have often been considered inappropriate for upscale wedding florals. But today's availability of hand-crafted, millinery-quality blossoms makes "silk" flowers exciting options. Their high quality is what makes them acceptable.

Rich velvets, shimmering satins, creamy silks, and organzas as thin as butterfly wings are used in crafting these botanicals that usually cost much more than their fresh counterparts. However, fancy fabric flowers are of "keepsake" value and can make appropriate gifts for the bridal party.

These nosegays add a turn-of-the-century flair to today's weddings. The soft luster of fabric petals is enchanting against many modern bridal fabrics.

Purple and lavender fabric lilacs (1) bring out-of-season luxury to fall fashions.

A nosegay of transparent petaled roses in sheer organza (2) is sprinkled with antique millinery berries and finished with a lush wide bow.

Pink cabbage roses (3) nestle tenderly in a silver tussie-mussie holder.

ALL PHOTOS THIS PAGE: MARK ROBBINS, COURTESY OF ELEGANT BRIDE

ABOVE LEFT: Fall blossoms, entwined by thin gold wire, make a stunning nosegay.

fancy fabrics

A bride holds a posy (OPPOSITE) of lemon-yellow fabric roses accented with antique amber milliner's berries.

Analgous colors and satiny textures (ABOVE RIGHT) create excitement in a bouquet of permanent pansies and peonies. Ribbon roses, formed from the same ribbon used for streamers, are added to the cascade.

A timeless romantic styling of regal garden roses (BELOW RIGHT) in sorbet colors seems so real everyone will sniff for their fragrance.

Celebration

S E T T I N G S

DANIEL RAY, COURTESY OF ELEGANT BRIDE

MARK ROBBINS, COURTESY OF ELEGANT BRIDE

DANIEL RAY, COURTESY OF ELEGANT BRIDE

for F A L L

MARK ROBBINS, COURTESY OF ELEGANT BRIDE

MARK ROBBINS, COURTESY OF ELEGANT BRIDE

DANIEL RAY, COURTESY OF ELEGANT BRIDE

amber waves

Although wheat is an unexpected decorative element at a wedding, its status as an icon of fall and its symbolism for wishes of prosperity make it an autumn shoe-in.

A three-tier cake (OPPOSITE) is dressed with buttery rose blossoms and hydrangea florets. Amber wheat added between the layers disguises the plastic pedestals.

Antique pastel-colored florals decorate the base of a bronzy metal finial (ABOVE) for a richly divergent centerpiece. Behind the centerpiece are stalks of Italian black-beard wheat displayed in a tall square glass cylinder.

ABOVE LEFT: Deep golden wheat positioned vertically in clear glass vases supplies a lovely textural interest appropriate to fall floral designs.

MARK ROBBINS, COURTESY OF ELEGANT BRIDE

MARK ROBBINS, COURTESY OF ELEGANT BRIDE

LEFT: A warm fall centerpiece is made with both fresh and preserved flowers and bundled wheat.

autumn bounty

Shades of lime and parchment-beige (OPPOSITE) fill out a lovely circular centerpiece. Decorating the moist floral foam wreath base are fresh and freeze-dried roses, clusters of starflowers, sprigs of wheat, callas, freesias and mahogany brown spheres fashioned out of lacquered vine.

Fresh autumn produce mixed with complementary florals (BELOW RIGHT) creates a contemporary still-life.

MARK ROBBINS, COURTESY OF ELEGANT BRIDE

harvest sheaves

Candelabra clad with columns of Italian black-bearded wheat (OPPOSITE) decorate a massive staircase. Fresh hydrangeas and freeze-dried roses are positioned at the sheaves' binding points, while rubber bands camouflaged with raffia hold the bundle securely.

A once unadorned brass wall sconce (ABOVE) is transformed by a beautifully illuminated plethora of dried grasses. Fresh salal leaves add a rich green contrast to the sheaf.

Remember, when combining dried grass with burning candles, protective glass globes must be used around the candles for safety.

MARK ROBBINS, COURTESY OF ELEGANT BRIDE

MARK ROBBINS, COURTESY OF ELEGANT BRIDE

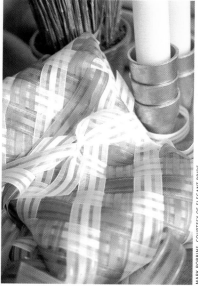

MARK ROBBINS, COURTESY OF ELEGANT BRIDE

golden highlights

The opulent golden tones of autumn become even more brilliant when given gilded highlights.

Natural and gold-painted stems of rye (OPPOSITE) create an interplay of color and texture. Bosc and Asian pears, skewered on dowel rods and placed in gilded pots, create a stacked and fruited candlestick.

Individual pears in gold pots (ABOVE) serve as place setting favors. Pears are sponged with metallic gold paint to enhance the effect.

ABOVE RIGHT: A sumptuous coordinating tablecloth is made by weaving creamy white and khaki gold striped satin and organza ribbons.

BELOW RIGHT: A pot of fragrant white roses and salal leaves tipped with gold paint is centered with a delicate ball candle.

MARK ROBBINS, COURTESY OF ELEGANT BRIDE

Winter
WEDDINGS

RUBRUM LILY • SPRAY ROSE • MING FERN • GLASS ORNAMENT • VELVET RIBBON • RUBRUM LILY

SPRAY ROSE • MING FERN • GLASS ORNAMENT • VELVET RIBBON • SPRAY ROSE • GLASS ORNAMENT

VELVET RIBBON • RUBRUM LILY SPRAY ROSE GLASS ORNAMENT • VELVET RIBBON

GLASS ORNAMENT • VELVET ING FERN • RUBRUM LILY

SPRAY ROSE • MING F UM LILY SPRAY ROSE

MING FERN • GLASS O NAMENT • VELVET

RIBBON • RUBRUM ET RIBBON • GLASS

ORNAMENT • VELVE RUBRUM LILY

SPRAY ROSE • MING FE LILY • SPRAY ROSE

MING FERN • GLASS O GLASS ORNAMENT • VELVET

RIBBON • RUBRUM LILY • SPRA SS ORNAMENT • VELVET RIBBON

GLASS ORNAMENT • VELVET RIBBON • RU SPRAY ROSE • MING FERN • RUBRUM LILY

SPRAY ROSE • MING FERN • GLASS ORNAM ET RIBBON • RUBRUM LILY • SPRAY ROSE

MING FERN • GLASS ORNAMENT • VELVET RIBB RAY ROSE • GLASS ORNAMENT • VELVET

RIBBON • RUBRUM LILY • SPRAY ROSE • MI ER SS ORNAMENT • VELVET RIBBON • GLASS

ORNAMENT • VELVET RIBBON • RUBRU LILY ROSE • MING FERN • RUBRUM LILY

VELVET RIBBON • SPRAY ROSE • GLASS OR MENT T RIBBON • RUBRUM LILY • SPRAY ROSE

MING FERN • GLASS ORNAMENT • VE T RIB GLASS ORNAMENT • VELVET RIBBON

Bouquets

SET THE MOOD

DANIEL RAY, COURTESY OF ELEGANT BRIDE

LON MURDICK, COURTESY OF ELEGANT BRIDE

DANIEL RAY, COURTESY OF ELEGANT BRIDE

for WINTER

Modern fashions require bouquets that are distinctive and equally up to date. Many of today's favorite bouquet styles are neatly structured and contain only one type of flower, like these rose cones.

The white roses in this conical bouquet (OPPOSITE AND RIGHT) accent and enhance the bride's ivory satin gown and echo the texture of the alençon lace panel in the skirt and on the sleeves.

Although almost any blossom can be used, roses are most effective and easy to build into the cone form. Rose varieties with slender stalks provide the flexibility necessary to hand tie conical bouquets.

Construction of this bouquet begins with the single topmost flower, then three blossoms are set slightly below and secured with florists' tape. Additional rows of roses are added in graduated levels until a cone shape is achieved.

The hand-held bouquets may be dropped into vases after the ceremony, providing attractive and convenient centerpiece arrangements.

MARK ROBBINS, COURTESY OF ELEGANT BRIDE

MARK ROBBINS, COURTESY OF ELEGANT BRIDE

ABOVE: The simple, neatly structured cone bouquet is a perfect complement to modern bridal fashions.

DANIEL RAY, COURTESY OF ELEGANT BRIDE

MARK ROBBINS, COURTESY OF ELEGANT BRIDE

neopolitan roses

The deep green silk taffeta of the bridesmaids' dresses (OPPOSITE) is enhanced with a rose cone bouquet in assorted hues of yellow, pink, and red. Blending colors in the bouquet with mixed varieties of roses gives the appearance of a casual gathering of roses from a cutting garden. Multiple streamers add delicate motion to the composition.

MARK ROBBINS, COURTESY OF ELEGANT BRIDE

MARK ROBBINS, COURTESY OF ELEGANT BRIDE

LON MURDICK, COURTESY OF ELEGANT BRIDE

winter white

Winter calls for the warm tones of cream, candlelight, and ecru. In an ethereal bundle of ruffles and ribbon, this elegantly simple bouquet (OPPOSITE PAGE AND BOTTOM RIGHT) features a trio of exotic cattleya orchids nestled into loops of rich satin ribbon. A lack of foliage gives it a decidedly modern appeal.

An inverted brass bell, outfitted with a piece of wet foam, ingeniously serves as the bouquet's holder (ABOVE LEFT AND ABOVE RIGHT). With a blend of scents as complex as the finest perfumes, this intriguing cluster of fragrant lilies-of-the-valley, roses, and aromatic mint is ideal with the understated elegance of today's dresses.

LON MURDICK, COURTESY OF ELEGANT BRIDE

White has been the traditional color for weddings since the time of Queen Victoria and is especially lovely for winter.

MARK ROBBINS, COURTESY OF ELEGANT BRIDE

lovely lilies

White lilies represent purity and sweetness in the old-fashioned language of flowers. Today they make ultra-clean statements accenting simple fashions.

The lily's smooth ivory petals, blushed with pink (OPPOSITE AND TOP RIGHT), are a striking natural contrast to their stems, which are wrapped in satin cording.

Oriental lilies and foliage (LEFT) form the grandest of cascade bouquets.

When designing with lilies, keep in mind that the fleshy blossoms are always thirsty. If the design requires the flowers to be out of water, assembly should occur at the last minute, and lily designs should be refrigerated until use.

Red roses, combined with holly and hypericum berries, form a sensational red bouquet for the yuletide ceremony. A silver tray of holly berry boutonnieres await a handsome groom's party.

christmas reds

The opulent ornament-encrusted bouquet (ABOVE LEFT) is filled with roses, holly berries, and sprigs of evergreen. Glass holiday ornaments reflect shadows and candlelight, making them especially suited for evening ceremonies.

Amaryllis, one of the most popular winter holiday flowers, is hand tied (LEFT) and decorated with a generous width of ribbon sparkling with metallic highlights.

Glamellias, stunning flowers (ABOVE RIGHT) first popular in the '40s during the glamour era of old Hollywood, are composite flowers made of gladiolas that have been re-formed into new flowers. Set on a permanent leafy stem gilded with gold, the cascading lines create an accent inspired by Asian minimalism.

MARK ROBBINS, COURTESY OF ELEGANT BRIDE

HERIBERT BREHM, COURTESY OF ELEGANT BRIDE

winter berries

An intense palette of saturated tones warms up to a crisp white gown (OPPOSITE AND ABOVE RIGHT). The tapestry of color in a compact bouquet of magenta and purple freesias, 'Leonidas' and 'Sabara' roses, ink blue veronica, cherry-red yarrow, maroon hypericum, aubergine privet berries, violet sea holly, glossy galax foliage, and variegated bush ivy provides the ultimate luxury.

A more simple version of the berried bouquet (ABOVE LEFT) is abundant with pink roses and hypericum berries.

LON MURDICK, COURTESY OF ELEGANT BRIDE

LEFT: Massed groupings of purple statice and stock form a diminutive nosegay for a simple velvet dress.

passionate purple

The color harmonies of lilac and purple create royal bouquets in many forms.

The tussie-mussie of fabric lilac blossoms (OPPOSITE) is a dense yet simple flower mass which is showcased beautifully against an equally simple gown.

In contrast to the spherical form of the lilac posy, the African violet cascade (ABOVE RIGHT) is perfect for heavy fabrics and laces. Blue hydrangeas, delphiniums, and saxicola surround the delicate African violet, and fresh ivy and romantic watercolored ribbons gently cascade from the elegant cluster. When preparing African violets for use in a bouquet, it's best to leave the plant intact by washing off the soil and wrapping the roots in plastic.

Boutonnieres

ADD DISTINCTION

1

2

According to legend, a young Prince Albert, in a spontaneous and quite romantic gesture, cut a small hole in his lapel with a pocket knife and slipped a rose from his bride's bouquet into the hole. Although the custom of buttonhole flowers or boutonnieres is older than this legend, the Victorian fable is certain to have revived their popularity.

Today's buttonhole flowers evoke elegant simplicity with attention to detail.

Try wrapping the stem of a preserved rose with ribbon (1) or gold beading wire like the cluster of white freesia (2) for a striking accent against black formalwear.

Likewise, loops of green ribbon create the appearance of silky foliage around a tender rose (3).

For a mixed collection, try a freesia blossom nestled in sprigs of statice and lavender for a fragrant touch (4) or combine sheer organza to a panicle of tiny kalanchoe blossoms (5).

Refined designs for the groom add the finishing touches to formalwear.

LON MURDICK, COURTESY OF ELEGANT BRIDE

OPPOSITE: The pinning of the buttonhole with stephanotises and holly berries. **ABOVE:** Hypericum berry boutonnieres in perfect condition at the end of the celebration.

3

4

for WINTER

5

Celebration
SETTINGS

MARK ROBBINS, COURTESY OF ELEGANT BRIDE

LON MURDICK, COURTESY OF ELEGANT BRIDE

MARK ROBBINS, COURTESY OF ELEGANT BRIDE

for WINTER

MARK ROBBINS, COURTESY OF ELEGANT BRIDE

MARK ROBBINS, COURTESY OF ELEGANT BRIDE

MARK ROBBINS, COURTESY OF ELEGANT BRIDE

LEFT: A grand staircase is lavishly adorned with traditional nosegays of 'Rendezvous' carnations, elaeagnus foliage, and wide luxurious bows. The nosegays on the staircase are designed in small foam cages and are wired to the banister along with rich Dior-like bows of wide purple satin. The attendant holds a coordinating hand-tied bouquet.

The venerable carnation, with its wide range of colors, sweet dependable fragrance, and long vase life, lends itself to a multitude of wedding designs. Breaking free of its stigma, this former signature flower of Napoleon Bonaparte makes a regal return to the wedding celebration.

An attendant's nosegay of 'Rendezvous' carnations (FAR LEFT AND ABOVE CENTER), hand-tied with a distinctive brown velvet and blue satin ribbon, is customized for the holidays with hypericum and green holly berries.

A sumptuous wreath of rich burgundy carnations (ABOVE LEFT AND ABOVE RIGHT) graces the front door. Elaeagnus foliage frames the carnations, encircling both the interior and exterior edges of the wreath. A wet foam wreath form will ensure a long life for these already hardy blossoms.

MARK ROBBINS

MARK ROBBINS, COURTESY OF ELEGANT BRIDE

MARK ROBBINS, COURTESY OF ELEGANT BRIDE

OPPOSITE: A mass of roses in tones of red encircles a potted maidenhair fern.

ABOVE LEFT: A design of cut amaryllises, roses, evergreen sprigs, and shimmering glass ornaments topped with delicate tapers are the perfect holiday touch for an evening dinner reception.

ABOVE TOP: An inverted mercury glass ornament topping a two-tier rose design, warmly brings the consummate garden gazing ball inside on a cold wintry day.

ABOVE: A classic wire-framed ivy topiary is encircled by red rose blossoms nestled in miniature gilded satellite pots.

LON MURDICK, COURTESY OF ELEGANT BRIDE

rose profusions

With romantic fragrances and vibrant colors, massed rose table designs stylishly evoke messages of love and luxury at formal or informal wedding receptions. Today's bride decorates with roses because they come in a variety of colors and are available year-round. Roses work well for many themes and mix with other flowers beautifully. For arrangements at the height of their beauty, use roses that are slightly open, or mix roses in several stages, from tight buds to fully open, for a garden-picked appearance. Romance is always in season with massed rose table designs.

MARK ROBBINS, COURTESY OF ELEGANT BRIDE

MARK ROBBINS, COURTESY OF ELEGANT BRIDE

LON MURDICK, COURTESY OF ELEGANT BRIDE

Apples and anemones and statice and stock combine to create an abundant centerpiece (OPPOSITE PAGE AND ABOVE LEFT) that mixes fruits and flowers together in a manner reminiscent of Colonial Williamsburg. In double rings around the edge of the container, fresh apples provide the base on top of which the ruffle-edged anemones are mounded. A layer of leafy salal and needled evergreens punctuated with purple statice creates a "collar" on which the fruit and flowers rest in this vivid table setting. Encircled by a collar of foliage and loops of opulent gold mesh ribbon (ABOVE CENTER), a sophisticated nosegay of 'Merry Widow' tulips is transformed into a glittering holiday bouquet.

ABOVE RIGHT: White roses subtly accent the fondant-covered wedding cake. The center petals of the roses have been removed to resemble open garden roses. Tucked among the bows of rolled fondant, the foliage-free roses almost appear to be made of the thick buttercream paste themselves.

MARK ROBBINS, COURTESY OF ELEGANT BRIDE

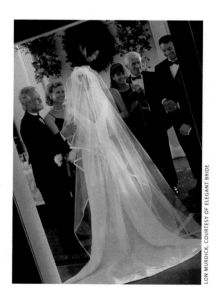

LON MURDICK, COURTESY OF ELEGANT BRIDE

sumptuous settings

'Privé' and 'Lavonde' roses, purple and white freesias, and fuchsia and royal blue cinerarias (OPPOSITE) provide an impressive palette against the stark white frosting. Inverted wine glasses are used to elevate the cake's tiers while the table is covered with multiple layers of crocheted lace.

The gracious pomander arrangement (ABOVE RIGHT) begins with water-soaked floral foam encased in a caging of chicken wire. Covered with red sweetheart roses, magenta Chinese carnations, and Christmas red and burgundy miniature carnations, this bouquet option is carried by a handle made from sheer ribbon. After the ceremony, the arrangement may be placed on a silver candlestick or vase for an easy reception arrangement.

The rich rose and holly berry pomander arrangement (ABOVE LEFT) is set on a silver candlestick for a touch of romance at the guest book table.

Fashioned atop an artful multistem trunk of curly willow branches, this sumptuous tabletop topiary is formed with varieties of roses in colors ranging from red to orange. Combined with heather and fresh plums, they create a vibrant analogous color harmony. The terra-cotta pots have been sprayed alternately with water and paint to give a moss-encrusted appearance.

MARK ROBBINS, COURTESY OF ELEGANT BRIDE

MARK ROBBINS, COURTESY OF ELEGANT BRIDE

FAR LEFT: The small pots of roses are great accents when placed elsewhere in the room.

LEFT: A tussie-mussie, casually laid aside by a bridesmaid, is a harmonious extension of the floral décor.

LON MURDICK, COURTESY OF ELEGANT BRIDE

rose topiaries

The Latin term *opus topiarium* was a general term for ornamental gardening. Topiary evolved into a term that represents any plant that has been trained to grow in a decorative manner. These floral arrangements presented in topiary fashion celebrate the heritage of the age-old tradition of decorative gardening–perfect for bringing a winter garden indoors for a holiday reception.

Glossary

Flowers
BY COLOR

White Flowers

Agapanthus	Hyacinth
Alstroemeria	Hydrangea
Amaryllis	Iris
Anemone	Lilac
Aster	Lily-of-the-valley
Baby's Breath	Lisianthus
Bouvardia	Magnolia
Calla	Narcissus
Camellia	Peony
Candy Tuft	Poinsettia
Carnation	Poppy
Cattleya Orchid	Queen Anne's Lace
Dahlia	Ranunculus
Daisy	Rose
Delphinium	Snapdragon
Dogwood	Star of Bethlehem
Euphorbia	Statice
Foxglove	Stephanotis
Freesia	Stock
Gardenia	Tuberose
Gerbera	Tulip
Gladiolus	Zinnia

Blue Flowers

African Violet	Hydrangea
Agapanthus	Iris
Ageratum	Larkspur
Ajuga	Lavender
Anemone	Limonium
Aster	Lisianthus
Brodiaea	Love-in-a-Mist
Campanula	Lupine
Cineraria	Monkshood
Clematis	Morning Glory
Columbine	Pansy
Cornflower	Phlox
Crocus	Primula
Delphinium	Salvia
Echinops	Scabiosa
Eryngium	Scilla
Exacum	Statice
Forget-me-not	Streptocarpus
Freesia	Veronica
Globe Thistle	Viola
Grape Hyacinth	Violet
Hyacinth	Wisteria

Pink Flowers

Alstroemeria	Hydrangea
Amaryllis	Ixia
Anthurium	Kalanchoe
Astilbe	Larkspur
Azalea	Lily
Bouvardia	Lisianthus
Calla	Nerine
Camellia	Peony
Campanula	Phlox
Carnation	Poinsettia
Chrysanthemum	Primula
Cornflower	Prunus
Cosmos	Ranunculus
Crocus	Rose
Cyclamen	Snapdragon
Dahlia	Stock
Freesia	Sweet Pea
Geranium	Sweet William
Gerbera	Tulip
Gladiolus	Violet
Godetia	Yarrow
Hyacinth	Zinnia

Purple Flowers

African Violet	Gomphrena
Allium	Heather
Alstroemeria	Iris
Anemone	Lavender
Aster	Liatris
Azalea	Lilac
Campanula	Lisianthus
Carnation	Pansy
Cattleya	Phalaenopsis
Chrysanthemum	Phlox
Cornflower	Physostegia
Cosmos	Primula
Crocus	Rose
Cyclamen	Scabiosa
Cymbidium	Statice
Dahlia	Stock
Delphinium	Sweet Pea
Dendrobium	Trachelium
Foxglove	Tulip
Freesia	Violet
Gladiolus	Wisteria
Godetia	Zinnia

Yellow Flowers

Acacia	Gerbera
Alstroemeria	Gladiolus
Begonia	Goldenrod
Black-eyed Susan	Hibiscus
Calla	Iris
Carnation	Ixia
Centaurea	Kalanchoe
Chrysanthemum	Lily
Clematis	Marigold
Cockscomb	Narcissus
Cosmos	Oncidium
Craspedia	Ranunculus
Crocus	Rose
Cymbidium	Sedum
Daffodil	Snapdragon
Dahlia	Solidago
Eremurus	Statice
Euphorbia	Sunflower
Fennel	Tansy
Forsythia	Tulip
Freesia	Yarrow
Genista	Zinnia

Peach Flowers

Alstroemeria	Gomphrena
Amaryllis	Hyacinth
Anthurium	Iris
Asclepias	Kalanchoe
Aster	Lily
Azalea	Nerine
Begonia	Poinsettia
Bourvardia	Poppy
Carnation	Primula
Chrysanthemum	Prunus
Clivia	Ranunculus
Cosmos	Rhododendron
Cymbidium	Rose
Dahlia	Sedum
Delphinium	Statice
Eremurus	Stock
Euphorbia	Sweet Pea
Genista	Sweet William
Geranium	Tulip
Gerbera	Watsonia
Gladiolus	Yarrow
Godetia	Zinnia

Flowers
BY SEASON

SPRING FLOWERS	Blue Lace	Cherry Blossom	Feverfew	Gypsophila
Acacia	Bluebell	Chrysanthemum	Forget-me-not	Heather
Allium	Bouvardia	Clematis	Forsythia	Honeysuckle
Alstroemeria	Brodiaea	Columbine	Foxglove	Hyacinth
Amaryllis	Calendula	Cornflower	Freesia	Iris
Anemone	Calla	Crocosmia	Gardenia	Ixia
Apple Blossom	Camellia	Crocus	Genista	Jonquil
Aster	Campanula	Cymbidium	Geranium	Kangaroo Paw
Astilbe	Candytuft	Daffodil	Gerbera Daisy	Larkspur
Azalea	Canterbury Bells	Daisy	Gipsy Bloom	Leptospermum
Baby's Breath	Carnation	Delphinium	Gladiolus	Liatris
Bachelor's Button	Caspia	Diosma	Godetia	Lilac
Bells-of-Ireland	Cattleya	Dogwood	Grape Hyacinth	Lily

Lily-of-the-valley
Love-in-a-mist
Lupine
Marguerite Daisy
Monkshood
'Monte Cassino' Aster
Narcissus
Orchid
Peach Blossom
Peony
Physostegia
Primrose
Pussy Willow
Queen Anne's Lace
Quince
Ranunculus
Rhododendron
Rose
Saponaria
Scabiosa
Snapdragon
Solidaster
Star of Bethlehem
Statice
Stephanotis
Stock
Strawflower
Sweet Pea
Sweet William
Tulip
Veronica
Violet
Watsonia
Waxflower
Yarrow

SUMMER FLOWERS
Agapanthus
Ageratum
Allium
Alstroemeria
Amaranthus
Amaryllis
Anemone
Anthurium
Artemisia
Aster
Astilbe
Baby's Breath
Bachelor's Button
Bells-of-Ireland
Bird-of-paradise
Blue Lace
Bottlebrush
Bouvardia
Brodiaea
Buttercup
Calendula
Calla
Campanula
Candytuft
Canterbury Bells
Carnation
Caspia
Cattleya
Centaurea

Chrysanthemum
Cockscomb
Columbine
Coreopsis
Cornflower
Cosmos
Crocosmia
Daisy
Delphinium
Echinops
Eremurus
Eryngium
Feverfew
Forget-me-not
Forsythia
Foxglove
Freesia
Fuchsia
Gardenia
Geranium
Gerbera
Gipsy Bloom
Gladiolus
Godetia
Gypsophila
Heather
Hollyhock
Honeysuckle
Hydrangea
Iris
Ixia
Jasmine
Kangaroo Paw
Larkspur
Lavender
Leptospermum
Liatris
Lilac
Lily
Lily-of-the-valley
Lisianthus
Love-in-a-mist
Lupine
Marco Polo
Marguerite Daisy
Marigold
Mock Orange
Monkshood
Montbretia
'Monte Cassino' Aster
Orchid
Pansy
Peony
Phlox
Physostegia
Primula
Protea
Queen Anne's Lace
Rhododendron
Rose
Safflower
Salvia
Saponaria
Scabiosa
Snapdragon
Snowball

Solidago
Solidaster
Star of Bethlehem
Statice
Stephanotis
Stock
Strawflower
Sunflower
Sweet Pea
Sweet William
Thistle
Tiger Lily
Trachelium
Tritoma
Tuberose
Veronica
Viola
Waxflower
Yarrow
Zinnia

AUTUMN FLOWERS
Allium
Alstroemeria
Amaranthus
Anemone
Artemisia
Aster
Baby's Breath
Bachelor's Button
Bells-of-Ireland
Bird-of-Paradise
Bittersweet
Bouvardia
Brodiaea
Calendula
Calla
Campanula
Candytuft
Carnation
Caspia
Cattleya
Centaurea
Chrysanthemum
Cockscomb
Coreopsis
Cornflower
Cosmos
Dahlia
Daisy
Delphinium
English Lavender
Feverfew
Forget-me-not
Foxglove
Freesia
Gardenia
Gerbera
Gipsy Bloom
Gladiolus
Gloriosa Lily
Godetia
Gomphrena
Gypsophila
Heather
Hydrangea

Iceland Poppy
Iris
Ixia
Kaffir Lily
Kale
Kangaroo Paw
Larkspur
Leptospermum
Liatris
Lily
Lily-of-the-valley
Lisianthus
Lunaria
Lysimachia
Marguerite Daisy
Marigold
Monkshood
Montbretia
'Monte Cassino' Aster
Nigella
Orchid
Pepperberry
Phlox
Physostegia
Protea
Pumpkin
Queen Anne's Lace
Ranunculus
Rose
Rose Hips
Rover
Rudbeckia
Safflower
Salvia
Scabiosa
Snapdragon
Solidago
Solidaster
Star of Bethlehem
Statice
Stephanotis
Stock
Strawflower
Sunflower
Sweet Annie
Sweet William
Thistle
Tuberose
Verbascum
Veronica
Violet
Yarrow
Zinnia

WINTER FLOWERS
Acacia
Allium
Alstroemeria
Amaryllis
Anemone
Baby's Breath
Bachelor's Button
Bells-of-Ireland
Bird of paradise
Bouvardia

Brodiaea
Calendula
Calla
Carnation
Caspia
Cattleya
Chrysanthemum
Cornflower
Cymbidium
Daisy
Delphinium
Diosma
Freesia
Gardenia
Gerbera
Gipsy Bloom
Gladiolus
Gypsophila
Heather
Hyacinth
Iris
Ixia
Kale
Larkspur
Leptospermum
Liatris
Lily
Lily-of-the-valley
Lisianthus
Longiflorum Lily
Madonna Lily
Marguerite Daisy
Monkshood
'Monte Cassino' Aster
Narcissus
Orchid
Poinsettia
Protea
Queen Anne's Lace
Quince
Ranunculus
Rose
Scabiosa
Snapdragon
Solidaster
Star of Bethlehem
Statice
Stephanotis
Stock
Sweet Pea
Sweet William
Trumpet Lily
Tulip
Waxflower

Flowers & Herbs

AND THEIR MEANINGS

A

Acacia ....Chaste Love
Alstroemeria...Aspiring
Amaryllis ....Pride, timidity, splendid beauty
Anemone (Garden) ....Forsaken
Aster (China) ....Variety, daintiness
Azalea...Temperance

B

Baby's Breath...Festivity
Bachelor's Buttons.......................................Anticipation
Basil ....Good wishes
Bay Leaf...I change but in death
Bittersweet ....Truth
Black-eyed Susan ....Encouragement
Bluebell..Constancy

C

Calla ....Aristocratic, regal
Camellia...Graciousness
Candytuft ....Indifference
Canterbury Bell .... Acknowledgement
Carnation, Pink.......................................Gratitude
Carnation, Red ....Flashy
Carnation, Striped ....Refusal
Carnation, White.................................Remembrance
Carnation, Yellow ....Cheerful
Chamomile ....Energy in adversity
China Aster ....Variety
Chrysanthemum, Bronze ....Excitement
Chrysanthemum, Red ....I love
Chrysanthemum, White ....Truth
Chrysanthemum, Yellow ....Slighted love
Clematis..Mental Beauty
Cockscomb...Foppery, affectation
Columbine..Folly
Coriander...Hidden worth
Cornflower...Delightful
Cosmos...Peaceful
Crocus ....Foresight

D

Daffodil..Regard, chivalry
Dahlia...Refined taste, dignity
Daisy, White..Innocence
Delphinium..Boldness
Dill ....Pizzazz
Dock ....Patience
Dogwood ....Durability

F

Fern ....Fascination
Forget-me-not.............Remember me forever, true love
Freesia...Spirited
Fuchsia, Scarlet ....Taste

G

Gardenia ....Joy
Geranium, Oak-leafed ....True friendship
Geranium, Rose-scented ....Preference
Gladiolus......................................Strength of character
Globe Amaranth..................Immortality, unfading love
Goldenrod ....Precaution

H

Hibiscus ....Delicate beauty
Holly...............................Foresight, domestic happiness
Hollyhock ....Ambition, fecundity
Honeysuckle..............Generous and devoted affection
Hyacinth...................................Sport, game, play
Hydrangea ....A boaster, heartlessness

I

Iris...................................Faith, hope, wisdom, and valor
Ivy ....Fidelity

J

Jasmine...Amiability
Jonquil...............................I desire a return of affection
Juniper......................................Succor, protection

L

Larkspur ....Lightness, levity
Laurel..Glory

Lilac...Humility
Lily, Day ....Coquetry
Lily, White..Purity, sweetness
Lily, Yellow..Falsehood, gaiety
Lily-of-the-valley ....Return of happiness
Lisianthus...Calming
Lotus ....Eloquence
Love-in-a-mist..Perplexity
Love-lies-bleeding.....................Hopeless, not heartless
Lupine................................Voraciousness, imagination

M
Magnolia ....Love of nature
Marigold ....Desire for riches
Mimosa (Sensitive Plant) ....Sensitiveness
Mint ....Virtue
Mistletoe.....................................I surmount difficulties
Morning Glory...........................Affection, superficial
Moss...Maternal love
Myrtle...Love

N
Narcissus.......................................Egotism, self-esteem
Nasturtium...Patriotism

O
Olive ....Peace
Orchid, Butterfly ....Sensitive love
Orchid, Cattleya ....Delicate beauty
Orchid, Cymbidium.....................Strength of character
Orchid, Japhet ....Joy
Oregano ....Boisterous

P
Pansy ....Loving thoughts
Parsley...Festivity
Peony...Happy marriage
Peppermint...Warmth of feeling
Phlox ....Unanimity
Poppy, Red...Pleasure
Poppy, White...................Sleep, my bane, my antidote
Primrose..I can't live without you

Q
Queen Anne's Lace............................Delicate femininity

R
Ranunculus ....You are rich in attractions
Rose ....Love
Rose, Helaborus ....Relieve my anxiety
Rose, Pink...Friendship
Rose, Red ....Passionate love
Rose, White..Purity

Rose, Yellow ....Decrease of love, jealously
Rosemary...Remembrance

S
Sage...Domestic virtue
Snapdragon ....Presumption
Snowball ....Bound
Spearmint ....Warmth of sentiment
Statice ....Success
Stephanotis ....Good luck
Stock...Lasting beauty
Sunflower ....Haughtiness
Sweet Basil ....Good wishes
Sweet Pea ....Blissful pleasure
Sweet Violet...Modesty
Sweet William ....Gallantry

T
Tansy ....Resistance
Thistle, Common...Austerity
Thyme ....Activity, vitality
Tuberose..Sensuality
Tulip ....Fame
Tulip, Pink ....Caring
Tulip, Purple..Royalty
Tulip, Red ....Declaration of love
Tulip, Variegated ....Beautiful eyes
Tulip, White ....Forgiveness
Tulip, Yellow ....Hopeless love

V
Veronica ....Fidelity
Violet, Blue...Faithfulness
Violet, Yellow.....................................Rural happiness

W
Water Lily ....Purity of heart
Wheat ....Prosperity

Y
Yarrow...Good health

Z
Zinnia...Thinking of you

Florists' Review Enterprises, Inc.